TO WALK AND NOT FAINT

36 Sehnsucht – desire

    a) nothing in the world can satisfy.

    b) nothing in the world can remove it – therefore –

    c) make for another world

To Walk and Not Faint

A Month of Meditations on Isaiah 40

SECOND EDITION

MARVA J. DAWN

WILLIAM B. EERDMANS PUBLISHING COMPANY
GRAND RAPIDS, MICHIGAN / CAMBRIDGE, U.K.

Previously published in 1980 as
To Walk and Not Faint: God's Comfort from Isaiah 40
by Christian Herald Books, Chappaqua, New York

Second edition
© 1997 Wm. B. Eerdmans Publishing Co.
255 Jefferson Ave. S.E., Grand Rapids, Michigan 49503 /
P.O. Box 163, Cambridge CB3 9PU U.K.

Printed in the United States of America

09 08 07 06 05 04 03   10 9 8 7 6 5 4 3

Library of Congress Cataloging-in-Publication Data

Dawn, Marva J.
    To walk and not faint : a month of meditations on Isaiah 40 / Marva J. Dawn
        p.   cm.
    Includes bibliographical references.
    ISBN 0-8028-4290-9 (pbk. : alk. paper)
    1. Bible.   O.T.   Isaiah XL — Meditations.   I. Title.
    BS1520.D38   1997
    224'.106 — dc21   97-4927
                                           CIP

to my parents,
who taught me to cry to God
and to hear God's cries —
and whose model of ministry
gave direction and purpose
to my life

Contents

CONTENTS

Introduction

The thought struck me while I was doing my usual swimming workout. As I considered the people around me in the pool, I yearned more than ever before for the Christian community to do a better job of transmitting to the society that surrounds us the appealing alternatives that we have been given. Our faith gives us profound resources to face all of life. Our relationship with God and his[1] revelation of himself in his Word enable us to handle every dimension of our existence, from the personal frustrations of our private lives to the frightening threats of global political and economic chaos.

These thoughts made me want to speak tenderly to everyone around me the good news of the hope and strength that are available to God's people. But most of the folks at the exercise club are generally too caught up in other things to care much

---

1. Out of my concern to reach the widest audience possible, I have chosen to refer to God with the pronouns, *he, his,* and *him,* which I have always understood as gender-neutral — and yet personal — when used in connection with God. I apologize to anyone who might be offended by my word choices and pray that you will accept my decision to use our inadequate language as carefully as possible for many kinds of people. Certainly God is neither masculine nor feminine, but more than all our words can ever connote.

about Christ and a life of faith. Many have not yet recognized their own cries of this life's emptiness, nor have they yet experienced the futility of life without God.

"A voice says, 'Cry!'" Isaiah 40 begins. "What shall I cry?" the prophet responded, and the voice gave him crucial messages to proclaim. Now, returning to rewrite this book more than fifteen years after its first printing, I continue to be struck by the way the whole fortieth chapter of Isaiah deals with so many of the momentous issues in today's society. Each verse challenges us with significant substance for life and a vital motivation for growth in discipleship. This book is designed to let you meditate on a verse from this profound chapter every day for a month — and yet we will have only begun to scratch the surface of its treasures.

Oh, the changes that take place in our lives as we grow to know God better! Each time we deeply study a verse from the Scriptures, God's Word reveals to us so much more of who he is. So I want to invite you to join me in contemplating God's relation to all the cries of our existence, in realizing how our relationship with him gives us unusual ability to handle all the dimensions of life.

Before we begin these studies, however, we need a bit of literary, structural, and theological background. The first thirty-nine chapters of the book of Isaiah are predominantly messages of warning and rebuke, doom oracles pronounced against various nations, including the chosen people of Israel. Occasionally, a song of Joy intrudes (most notably in chapters 12 and 35), and many of the most significant prophecies concerning the Messiah (for example, 7:14; 9:2-7; and 11:1-10) appear in this first part of the book. However, the major mood of these thirty-nine chapters is denunciatory; the style is terse.

Suddenly, however, the mood and style change. After three historical chapters recording again the siege of Sennacherib against Jerusalem in 701 B.C.E. and the illness of King Hezekiah (almost identical to the account in 2 Kings 18–20), the fortieth chapter of Isaiah shifts dramatically to intense poetry of stirring majesty and empowering comfort.

After the warning and denunciation, hope breaks through. After the Babylonian captivity, which the people of Israel suffered because they turned to the gods of money and power and away from the true LORD of all, the sovereign God enabled them to return home to Zion. The theological movement is the same for all of us: After the law shows us our sin and need for deliverance, the gospel frees us from our captivities and brings us home to God. Isaiah 40 is like a springboard — thrusting us into the flight of the eagle, catapulting us into trust.

That brief background will have to suffice, for this book is not intended as a commentary or a theological tome, but rather as one example of how we can read the narratives of the Scriptures to form our character as believers and as a community of faith. For that reason, the book will not get bogged down in disputed histori-cal-critical and redactional issues of dating and authorship and connections to the first half of the book of Isaiah, for these argu-ments prevent us from letting the text challenge us, change us, care for us. Rather, my approach is more canonical and literary — paying attention to the Bible as metanarrative (i.e., overarching, universal story) and noting the literary devices of the poet — in order that my approach can be, above all, devotional.

I first learned to read the Bible as story, the grand story of a God who cares for his people with an everlasting and par-ticular love, during my first graduate training in English literature. But my most important training for this kind of reading of the text came in my childhood, when I learned from my parents that the best thing in all of life is to love and serve God and glorify him forever. To that end, may the words in this book deepen not only your knowledge of God but, more important, your adoration.

It is my hope that these devotional meditations on the

text may enable us to grow in our living relationship with the LORD for whose coming we are called to prepare. We will dwell deeply in this single chapter of Isaiah 40 in order to focus intensively on all the cries it contains. Each meditation will observe carefully what the text says, consider some of the nuances and implications of the original Hebrew, and recognize how our lives fit into the bigger story of the biblical narrative. I pray not only that you will benefit from these particular meditations on Isaiah 40, but also that this book might offer you new skills or strengthen your existing skills for similar meditations on other scriptural passages.

Let me explain a few conventions followed in this book. The chief character of these pages is the LORD as he reveals himself to his people. I have followed the customary practice in Bibles of capitalizing all the letters in the words *LORD* and *GOD* when the Hebrew word to be translated is the name *YHWH*,[2] which is often vocalized as *Yahweh* (formerly as *Jehovah*). That is the name by which the LORD revealed himself to Moses at the burning bush in Exodus 3:14-15. It is a term that distinguishes him from all the neighboring, false deities. He is not just a god, but he alone is the faithful covenant God, the great "I AM."

2. The original Hebrew noun was composed of these four consonants, Y H W H, which relate to the root of the verb "to be." Since the Jews honor God's name by not saying it aloud (for fear that they might blaspheme it) and since the original Hebrew manuscripts were written with only consonants and not the vowel points, scholars are not sure how to say the word. Rather than rendering the word with a suggested pronunciation, I will use *YHWH* in this book with the hope that this will cause you to reflect upon its mystery and God's unreachable majesty. It seems to me that our postmodern times suffer from a lack of awe and reverence and "fear" for God. I put the word *fear* in quotation marks because I don't mean "terror," but I do intend a profound realization of our unworthiness before God so that we do not take God's gracious love and steadfast mercy for granted, as if we deserved it or could earn it or pay it back.

Throughout the First Testament[3] the name *YHWH,* the
LORD, implies the faithfulness of GOD, especially as he delivers
his people. We need to recover this image in our times, to learn
the glory of the LORD's constant faithfulness to his covenant and
his effective deliverance of his people from all their captivities.

It is also my custom to capitalize characteristic words at
points when I want to call attention to the difference in these
entities if they come directly from God and our relationship with
him (words such as *Truth* and *Joy*). That way the specific Joy of
the LORD, for example, can be easily distinguished from mere
(and fading) human happiness.

I pray that you might experience that Joy as you read the
pages that follow and meditate on the stirring narratives and gifts
that we as God's people have been given to tell and offer others.
A voice keeps saying, "Cry!"

3. I prefer to call the first three-fourths of the Bible the "First Testament" or the "Hebrew Scriptures," to avoid our culture's negative connotations
of the name *Old* Testament and to emphasize both the continuity of the
covenants in the Bible and also the consistency of God's grace for his people.

1 God's Cry of Comfort

"Comfort ye, O comfort my people,"
   says your God.

Isaiah 40:1 (composite)[1]

Where in the world can you and I find comfort and relief in the tough situations of life? Your company is downsizing, and suddenly your job of twenty years has evaporated. Your husband suddenly seems so distant and drifting still further away. You and your spouse can't figure out what to do about a son or daughter who is becoming rebellious. Maybe you wonder why you can't get past the depression that engulfs you. Who will ease the stabbing tensions of our lives, or who can alleviate the dull, throbbing ache of loneliness?

Perhaps despair is your constant companion. Even if you aren't feeling it now, you can remember times when you felt totally

---

1. Biblical quotations in this book are generally from the New Revised Standard Version. Sometimes other translations or a composite of several translations will be used to capture the original Hebrew more accurately.

helpless. Possibly dating relationships keep breaking down, or you feel unremittingly inadequate in the face of rapid changes at your workplace. Perhaps you anticipate even more difficult times as your children face temptations of drugs and sex, as your job gets more competitive and hectic. At one time or another, we all feel so overwhelmed by our situations that we grope for any fragment of comfort to sustain us.

Where in the world can comfort be found?

The situations described in the book of Isaiah were no better. Isaiah himself rebuked the Israelites for losing sight of their purpose as the chosen people. Intrigue and rebellion, hypocritical worship and injustice, materialism and idolatries of all sorts — the same sins plagued the people in his time as plague the world today. Then the Israelites were taken into captivity; their temple was destroyed, and the capital city's walls were torn down. Now Abraham's descendants were overcome with despair. Were they still God's chosen people? How could the LORD have let this happen to them? How could they be delivered from the Babylonians? When would they return to their own land?

After many chapters filled with doom oracles for other nations and rebukes for Israel, the fortieth chapter of Isaiah suddenly ushers in an entirely different tone. In the midst of the darkness of sin and despair, God proclaims a new message of light and hope. Similarly, in the midst of the troubled times of our personal lives and into the shambles of postmodern culture (that in despair has given up the modern myth of progress), God calls to his people today to hear new assurance, a word of comfort and victory.

" 'Comfort ye, O comfort my people,' says your God," the fortieth chapter begins. "That's easy to say," we might respond, "but is it real?"

"Comfort, O comfort." God says it twice to the nameless audience. One call to comfort is not enough, for pain and suffering are deep and agony is long. The fact that the verb occurs twice

2

implies that the comfort we are being offered is continuous. There IS comfort to be given, God declares.

The old King James Version captures better the plural form of this verb when it translates the imperative, "Comfort ye, comfort ye." (Perhaps a Southern version — "comfort y'all" — would capture its essence even better.) The prophet was not the only one called to offer solace to those who grieve or doubt or fear. This verse reaches out of the pages of our Bibles to call you and me to the ministry of comforting. The repetition of the verb reminds us that our nurturing and caring can be continuous as well. There is plenty of comfort for us to receive and to give.

Not only is there a bounteous supply, but what we receive and give is truly comforting. The world offers its solace, but it has no substance. Its words are hypnotic, but they do not heal. Society would comfort us with false hopes by feeding our egos or nursing our grudges or building our illusions. God, on the other hand, wants to give us the comfort of his Truth, the entire Truth concerning both our condition in relation to him and his gracious remedies for our brokenness.

Many years ago, in the first of what has turned out to be a twenty-year series of health crises, some of my well-meaning friends offered me nothing but human comfort. They attempted to cheer me with such comments as "It will be all right," or "A lot of people suffer severe illnesses," or "Soon you can go back to living a normal life."

The problem with those words was that they had no basis, no substance, no reality. Things may turn out all right, but at that moment, in a time of pain, it did not seem that way. Nor did the company of others going through the same experience make it any easier for me in that period of crisis. In fact, those statements made me feel all the more guilty; I knew I should trust God and rest in his grace, but the pain remained. I couldn't deny my feelings, and I couldn't silence my guilt about them. The last of those supposed words of comfort contradicted my doctor's opinion and so discouraged me all the more.

On the other hand, the president of the congregation I was serving at the time offered these words of genuine comfort: "The LORD is with you, and I care." That was truly a consoling declaration. What a sweet comfort it is to be reminded in the midst of pain and grief and guilt that God is there beside us, inside us, not condemning, to give us his everlasting solace! Words of comfort from a human perspective will pass away, but the truth about our eternal, unchanging, and caring Father will continue to abide and to offer comfort that endures.

The second phrase of verse 1 emphasizes the intimacy of this comfort. God commands his listeners to comfort "my people." The LORD's comfort is effective and personal because he has chosen to make us his people. We are not left stranded in a confused world, torn by circumstances or adrift in a sea of meaninglessness. God has a particular interest in what happens to each of us. And not only does he care, but he also has the power to do something about it all (as we shall discuss later).

God is sovereignly gracious. He really does love each one of us as a very important individual in his eternal plans. Therefore, we can know that no matter what the circumstances, no matter how frequently we fail to trust him, God wants to fill our lives with his deepest Joys and perfect Peace.

We ARE God's people. The biblical narrative enfolds us in the story of the Father thoroughly demonstrating his care for us through the life of his Son and sealing us as his own with the gift of the Holy Spirit. If we have been given these gifts of his grace, will he not also freely give us everything else that we truly need (Romans 8:32)?

The third phrase of this first verse drives the point home. We are not called to offer comfort just because we feel like it, but rather because that is what YHWH says. God's revelation about himself declares his comforting purposes. The phrase "says your God" carries with it an immense authority. The entire biblical canon displays how God will do what he says. Consequently, when we seek to pass on his solace to someone else, we can know that we are really giving it to her. It will indeed be available for her to receive. The Word of the LORD never comes back void, we are told elsewhere in the book of Isaiah, but always accomplishes the purposes for which it was sent (Isaiah 55:10-11).

The implications of these three phrases take two very important directions in our lives — one for ourselves and one for our relationships with others. Personally, we can look for the ways in which God will bring this word of consolation to us in whatever situations we might be confronting. Rooted in the authority of his Word and in God's call for us to be his own, we can be sure of his consolation in our trials, of his hope in our despair, of his peace in our confusion, and of his faithful presence in our bad times and good times.

For others, we have the capability, because of what we have learned from God, to offer deep and meaningful solace. We can assure them that God is a Father who speaks graciously to his children continuously. When we meet people who need hope and assurance, we do not have to settle for sentimental drivel or pious platitudes. We can give them solid comfort, consolations that are genuine and eternal — and free, out of the richness of God's most abundant grace.

What kind of comfort do you offer to those who need to hear consolation? What do you say, for example, to the good friend whose father just died, to the neighbor who can't keep up with the speed of life, to your wife who was bypassed for a promotion?

What kind of comfort do you carry with you into the uncomfortable situations of your life? What sustains you when circumstances beyond your control prevent your earning an adequate income, when you find yourself failing as a pastor, when you realize that your husband doesn't really love you anymore?

The chapters that follow explore many dimensions of God's inclusive grace and tender comfort. Here we begin by simply recognizing that God's comfort is real and that it is really for us all. To you, also, this sure word is addressed: " 'Comfort ye, O comfort my people,' says your God."

QUESTIONS FOR FURTHER MEDITATION:

It is not possible for me to address these verses from Isaiah 40 to the specific situations of your own life. Since I can't know what your particular needs and struggles might be, I invite you to take a closer look at this book's chapters as they relate to you by means of questions at the end of each meditation. Not all of the questions will be helpful to you. Please ignore those that don't seem helpful, but take time to ponder those that are useful; talk them over with your neighbor; discuss them in a Bible study group at your church or place of work. As I write, I pray that you will find specific comfort and deep Joy in your relationship with God as you meditate upon his Word and grow to know him better.

1. *How have I experienced the difference between the vain comfort the world gives and the everlastingly real comfort to be found in the* LORD?

2. *Why does the Word of God bear so much authority?*

3. *Why is it important to me that I, personally and individually, am one of God's people?*

4. *By what means can I offer God's comfort rather than the world's to my friends in need?*

5. *What kind of comfort does God offer in this mixed-up and frightening postmodern culture, when war and ethnic cleansing,*

famine, turmoil, the sterility of our technicized culture, meaningless-ness, and depersonalization threaten from every side?

6. *What are some favorite Bible verses that give special comfort in times of distress? (Some examples could be Lamentations 3:22-33, Psalms 27 and 34, and Habakkuk 3:17-19, as well as these verses in Isaiah 40.)*

7. *What are some of the aspects of the character of God implied by this verse and my study of it, and how can the knowledge of these characteristics be comforting to me?*

2 *The Cry of Release*

"Speak to the heart of Jerusalem,
  and call out to her
that her warfare [hard service] has ended,
  that her penalty of iniquity [is] accepted as paid off, forgiven
that she has received of the LORD's hand
  double for all her sins."

Isaiah 40:2 (New American
Standard, with sidenotes)

He had plagiarized his paper for my Literature of the Bible
course at the university. I had read the booklet from which
he stole his material just the week before; otherwise I might not
have caught it, since he was a good student. When I called him
into my office and told him what I knew, he visibly trembled.
"What can I do?" he asked.

"I should flunk you," I responded, "but first tell me what
caused you to plagiarize when you're entirely competent without
cheating." He told me of severe family expectations, peer pressure,
his need to be perfect. I spoke to his will. "I will forgive you, but

8

this paper still needs to be written — and it must be a longer one now. I believe you can do a great job."

"Speak to the heart," verse 2 begins in the original Hebrew. For the Jews, the word *heart* meant more than simply feelings. The word connotes the will and conscience, the intentions, inner person, and desires that are a combination of knowledge, emotion, and the passion of commitment. In moments of crisis, it is not enough to react merely with feelings. This larger sense of the "heart" helps us know how to speak most tenderly, for it is more than emotions that need healing.

Sometimes anguish wells up so powerfully, the pain in us seems so overwhelming, that we are sure it will break us apart with grief. When we've been deceived by someone we love, when a goal toward which we've been groping in a long struggle proves unattainable in the end, we need to find the will to surmount our feelings, to forgive, to go on toward different goals.

For the people of Israel, the overwhelming anguish was their captivity in Babylon because of their injustice and pride and idolatries. They were a rebellious nation and repeatedly ignored the rebukes and warnings of Isaiah, Jeremiah, and other prophets. Yet the LORD now commands, "Speak to the heart" — the will and intentionality — "of Jerusalem." After the captivity the Israelites needed words of hope, the will to return, promises to sustain them in the difficulties of beginning again. Consequently, *YHWH* addresses their minds and moral character.

Verse 1 commanded the unnamed listeners to "comfort my people." Now verse 2 adds the verbs "speak to the heart" and "call out" (also both plural) to complete the three-part command. Frequently in the book of Isaiah imperatives or descriptions are grouped in threes, a Hebrew means of underscoring the divinity of the set. These are tasks God himself summoned the Israelites to do, a trio of ministries to which God's people are still called in our times. We bring comfort, we speak to the wills and passions of others, and we cry out God's truths. We console others by addressing their inner person and by declaring to them the good news of grace that gives them the courage to go on.

Each of the commissions in this trio helps to define the others. We would not "speak to the heart" of another without an ultimate goal to comfort. Our crying out of truth requires sensitivity and tenderness. Our messages will come from the character of God, who is loving and gracious. Our words will be appropriate to the sufferings of the times, to meet others' deepest needs.

In this age of "if it feels good, do it," Christians who want their lives to be formed by the biblical narratives need exhortations to the will. We expect to hear the truths of God so that we can act on them. Especially we yearn for the Truth of God's forgiveness to give us fortitude to start over when we have blown it, when our own rebellions have led to well-deserved sufferings as inherent consequences.

After the opening three plural imperative verbs, verse 2 underscores the emphasis on divinity by offering another set of three — this time a set of gracious proclamations concerning the Israelites' situation. The message they receive is composed of these three elements: that Jerusalem "has served her term, that her penalty is paid, that she has received from the LORD's hand double for all her sins" (NRSV). Meditation on these three elements will enable God's people then and now to gain better perspective on their suffering.

First, we are told that the warfare of the people of God is over. In the time of the book of Isaiah, this primarily promised a physical end to the long, hard term of captive service. However, as all the prophets of Israel show, a message of freedom from hard labor is needed for all the struggles of our lives. We turn many of our jobs and situations into harder service than necessary because we try to live apart from God's grace. We live to earn human (and divine?) approval; we often place ourselves under "performance expectations" that are impossible to meet.

The call of Isaiah 40 that the term of hard service is over prefigures the even greater shout from the cross on Good Friday that the warfare had been ended and the debt paid. Christ brought to the finish the fight against all false expectations and human justifications and against all the powers of sin, evil, and death. His resurrection, ascension, and sending of the Holy Spirit forever carry that victory into the daily lives of his people. Indeed, the warfare ended once and for all when the Accuser was eternally and unalterably defeated at Golgatha.

Far too often, though, God's people live as if we still need to justify our own existence, to prove ourselves again from the beginning, to win God's grace. Daily we need to hear the exultant cry that the warfare is ended. Could we not, in the Christian community, more consistently help each other to realize afresh the thorough significance of that cry — that God has made it possible for us to rest in him?[1]

Of course, our freedom from justifying ourselves does not mean that we are not actively involved in living out our Christian commitment. Here, however, we are dealing with the strange paradox of the Christian life — namely, that we are actively involved in following Christ, but that it is the Spirit within us who makes that following possible and carries it out through our freedom.

Our own guilt is one of the greatest barriers to enjoying the freedom of the gospel. That barrier is smashed, however, by the

---

1. See especially chapter 8, "Spiritual Rest," in Marva J. Dawn, *Keeping the Sabbath Wholly: Ceasing, Resting, Embracing, Feasting* (Grand Rapids: Wm. B. Eerdmans, 1989), pp. 55-64. (I will occasionally footnote my other books to encourage you to pursue topics more thoroughly. Since the royalties are all given away to ministries that help the poor, your extended reading will also support this aid.)

second of the three proclamations to be called out to Jerusalem —
that is, that her iniquity has been removed. Her guilt has been
pardoned and her punishment accepted because of the immensity
of God's grace. We in New Testament times know better how that
can be true, for we know the fullness of Christ's love for us
throughout his life and work and death. The cry from the cross
recorded in John 19:30, *tetelestai* ("It has been finished"), was the
word marked on a debtor's bill when it was finally fully paid.

There is tremendous freedom in knowing that our iniquity
has been pardoned. Once we fully realize that our failures have
been forgiven, we can begin to put into effect these words from
Paul: "Forgetting what lies behind and straining forward to what
lies ahead, I press on" (Philippians 3:13b-14a). His exultant claim
contrasts with our typical downward cycles, in which our guilt
and remorse lead to more unwise actions or undesirable behavior,
which causes us to feel more guilty, which causes us to respond
even more poorly, and so on. Food and alcohol, drug and sex
addictions are often goaded by such guilt spirals.

One of my friends struggled constantly with the agony of
such a debasing loop. He was an extremely gifted young pianist
who had enormous trouble forcing himself to practice. Then he
would feel so guilty about his failures that his work sessions didn't
go well, which made it all the more difficult for him to motivate
himself to keep up the disciplines he knew were necessary. The
cruel consequence was a heavier burden of guilt.

The only way such a plunging spiral can be reversed is if it
is stopped short. The message of comfort in Isaiah 40:2 is just such
a cycle-stopper. Iniquity has been removed! God's child is freed by
that news to begin moving in an upward revolution, rejoicing in
forgiveness and working well because of the freedom of spirit that
God's gracious pardon produces. What Joy there can be when the
message of forgiveness is profoundly believed and actually lived!

The last phrase in verse 2 is ambiguous. It does not tell

us of *what* Israel has received double. Former interpreters and present translators have tended to associate the phrase with punishment for Israel's sins, but the literary context of the phrase has caused me to question that interpretation. Since this is a message of comfort and since the previous phrases recorded God's forgiveness, perhaps this ambiguous phrase is meant to refer to the LORD's grace. Certainly it was purely by grace that Israel was released from captivity — and by grace that God delivers us from the bondages into which we place ourselves.

Since the Hebrew word usually translated "received" in our versions is otherwise rendered "taken" (as a gift), the implication might be that Israel has accepted double pardon for all her sins. Truly, human beings could never suffer enough really to pay double in punishment for our sins, but the LORD's hand does offer grace freely and fully and more than doubly. The verse seems to end expectantly. We eagerly await what will happen next — and are quickly greeted with a new call to prepare for the revealing of the glory of *YHWH*.

At least three distinct episodes mark fulfillments of this verse. First, what a powerful work of grace it took to deliver the Israelites from their captivity, which was the result of their own idolatries and injustices. Yet in their repentance the faithful received the fulfillment of all God's promises to which they had clung during their ardent waiting to return from Babylon.

Second, the women and disciples waited in agony and darkness as Jesus finished his lifelong work of obedient holiness even to death on the cross — and they waited again on Easter morning until the truth of his resurrection was made clear. Though there is a lot of scholarly debate in contemporary theology about the precise meaning of the "atonement," the New Testament witnesses record these same three themes (as in Isaiah 40:2) in reference to Christ's work of reconciliation on our behalf — that through it our warfare to justify ourselves has ended, our penalty

13

of iniquity has been accepted as paid off, and we have received from the LORD's hand complete pardon for all our sins.

Finally, all creation groans in longing for the final revealing of God's double grace when Jesus comes again at the end of time. This final waiting will surely be the easiest, if we can remember more often that we already know the ultimate outcome. The ending of our existence as struggling, broken persons has been assured by Christ's triumphant victory cry. The principalities and powers have been exposed and defeated. The last enemy, death, has been annihilated.

There doesn't have to be any doubt. The warfare is ended, the guilt is removed, the grace is doubled. What good news to speak tenderly to someone's heart and will!

QUESTIONS FOR FURTHER MEDITATION:

1. In what situations have I lacked the will to go on, and what gave me new courage?

2. What kinds of hard service continue to engage my energies?

3. How could I learn to experience more thoroughly the victory over struggles, the ending of the term of hard service that Christ makes available to me in the sureness of his forgiveness?

4. What sources of guilt could I turn over to Christ to end the cycles of remorse and despair that cause me trouble?

5. How does grace break through for me?

6. How might I help someone else overcome the cycles of guilt and despair?

7. How do the three verbs — "comfort," "speak to the heart," "call out" — challenge me to minister to the people around me?

3 The Cry for Us to Prepare

A voice cries out:
"In the wilderness prepare the way of the LORD,
make straight in the desert a highway for our God."
Isaiah 40:3

The preparations took all day, but my friend's surprise was worth it. He had been kidding me by answering "Baked Alaska" every time I asked him for a suggestion of something special he might like to eat. So for his birthday I decided to make one. I invited several friends, baked the cake and froze it, packed the ice cream into a foil-lined bowl and later unmolded it on top of the cake, prepared the egg whites for the meringue. In the last moments the ice cream and cake were sealed inside a meringue shell, and the whole tray was put into a 500 degree oven. It worked! When we cut the slices of Baked Alaska, the meringue was nicely browned, and the ice cream was still frozen. My friend was delighted. The magic of the "unveiling" was worth the effort.

Imagine how infinitely worthwhile will be the Joy of the unveiling anticipated by this third verse. After the promise of the first two verses, verse 3 continues with the command to prepare. The comfort that is coming is so good that we are now stirred up to get ready to receive it. The preparations will be tremendously worthwhile, for the glory of the LORD himself is going to be revealed (see verse 5).

This verse's images reminded the Israelites of their first trip through the wilderness after their release from slavery in Egypt. (The book of Isaiah contains numerous phrases reminiscent of that deliverance.) Then this verse was fulfilled and the glory of *YHWH* was revealed in the desert when they were able, miraculously, to return from Babylon. The difficulties of contemporary refugees who are permitted to return to their homes might give us a glimpse of both the great gladness and the mingled fears for the future that accompanied that return. The Hebrew people could gather courage if they knew it was *YHWH*'s way, God's highway, they traveled.

John the Baptizer applied this verse to himself when he announced the coming of Jesus, the Christ. Describing the function of his preaching, he declared himself to be the one designated to prepare the way of the LORD. He was the fulfillment of this verse in a second sense — but a third fulfillment applies to us. In our time, too, we are to be preparers.

The phrase that begins this verse actually means, "A voice is heard calling." In verse 2 this same Hebrew verb occurred in the imperative form, "cry out." Now it occurs in the form of a participle to indicate that a voice making a proclamation keeps continuing to be heard. The text does not say whose voice it is or where it comes from. We only know that the voice is heard and that it commands whoever listens to clear the way for the LORD. The prophets of Israel, the Hebrew people, John the Baptizer, and we Christians today should make smooth in the desert a highway for our God.

How can we prepare the way for *YHWH*? How do we

16

make straight a highway for our God? The second Hebrew verb in the voice's command is intensive: "cause to be straight." There are many ways in which you and I who hear this voice can cause the road to be made straight, to ready ourselves and others for God's coming.

For example, how do we prepare our minds and souls for God to enter them more deeply now? The way was prepared for Jesus to come the first time when John the Baptizer stirred up Jewish listeners to repent and to long for the Kingdom of God. When Jesus returns, the Scriptures say, the way will be prepared gloriously — with the sounding of trumpets, the raising of the dead, the heralding of the hosts of heaven. What should we do now? How do we construct in the wilderness a highway for the LORD?

The graphic imagery of this text challenged the Israelites to remove those obstructions that stood in the way and prevented the LORD's coming. Certainly our hearts are often like a barren and stony wilderness. The figure suggests the driest desert, windswept and waterless, an apt characterization of a life withered in its self-centeredness. To that emptiness God wants to come, bringing us streams of living water (John 7:38).

It's not that we could work to deserve his coming. It's not that by our efforts we make that coming possible. The problem is that God wants to come more richly into our lives, but is often prevented by the obstructions we keep building or by our failure to open ourselves to his gifts.

What kinds of things obstruct God's way? For some, the path is blocked by fears; for others, the obstruction is pride or our illusions of our own importance, deceptive opinions of our own ability to handle things by ourselves. The path might be blocked by our mistaken anger at God — when we blame him inaccurately for not interrupting life's natural processes and consequences.

17

During my college years I visited the wilderness of Judea and was astounded by its bleakness and desolation. I saw in that wilderness the terror of shifting sands that whirled with the winds and completely hid the highway. They blinded my eyes and stung my skin.

Our own lives can be seas of shifting sands of perplexities. The winds of time and change blow everything around and confuse us. We lose our way by falling prey to peer pressures and societal currents alien to the Kingdom of God. It is so much easier to go with the flow than to live as the alternative community on God's strange highway. How can we find the courage to be odd? How can this task of preparing be fulfilled?

The message of the voice that cries is a stark reminder of our absolute need for God to empower us for all of life. We can't prepare the way for him except by his grace. We can't clean out the obstructions; we can't make the way open except as God does it in us and through us. This third verse calls us to our knees in humble repentance, and it calls us to adoration as we thank God for the grace given so abundantly to work for us, in spite of us.

John the Baptizer knew that this was the way to fulfill the call to prepare the way for Jesus to come. His entire task in life was to urge people to repent in order to receive the forgiveness of sins.

Similarly, this verse calls us to repentance, and we, in turn, can invite others to contrition also. One of the great gifts of the Christian community is the opportunity to remind each other of the need for confession and of the certainty of forgiveness, the need for constant vigilance in the wildernesses of our lives. Together we can recognize and repent of the obstructions we put there. It is the LORD himself who wants to come and who promises to enable us to prepare the way.

We can take the imagery of this verse a step further. Not only do we allow things to block God's coming, but also, neglecting our spiritual lives, we let ourselves become scorched and *hunger and thirst for righteousness*

made dry and barren. Our hearts have become a wilderness because they have not been cultivated. In the desert of our lives, desperate for approval and empty in spite of affluence, we are called to prepare the way for the LORD. The cry to make a highway invites us to the disciplines of cultivation — nourishing our minds with God's Word, watering the stoniness with worship, raking away the rocks by the admonition of fellow Christians.

There can be no other response to this verse than for us to have a greater desire to make the way more open. God is ready and waiting to come more richly into our lives. The way can be made clear by our devoting time to be with him, meditating on his Word, listening to this voice proclaiming, engaging in prayer, and hearing the calls of other members of his Kingdom. Our disciplines cannot earn us his presence, but they cultivate the way for him to come.

This, too, is all made possible by God's grace. Nothing can be done except as he draws us. No hunger is stirred up in our hearts unless God himself stirs it up. So we listen to the voice, and God uses that attention. We are invited to join the ranks of the prophets, John the Baptizer, and the seventy whom Jesus sent out two by two to prepare the way in all the cities to which he himself was about to go (Luke 10). We are sent now to be God's agents for stirring up one another in the community of faith and in the world.

QUESTIONS FOR FURTHER MEDITATION:

1. Through what means do I hear the voice calling yet today?

2. What sins have I allowed to obstruct the way of the LORD's coming more deeply into my life?

3. What cultural influences cause the sands to shift and obstruct the highway?

4. What means do I use to cultivate the wilderness of my own life?

5. How can I help others to remove obstructions or to cultivate their lives?

6. What will it mean to me if God comes more fully into my life?

7. What might it mean for my local congregation if God comes more fully into our community?

4 *The Cry to Remove Obstructions*

"Every valley shall be lifted up,
and every mountain and hill be made low;
the uneven ground shall become level,
and the rough places a plain."

Isaiah 40:4

It is a typical professional hazard for those who serve in the Church that we frequently find ourselves drowning in discouragement. One of the worst periods of demoralization for me came when a grossly unfair review of two of my books appeared in a conservative journal. The reviewer not only completely misconstrued both books, but also leveled numerous personal attacks in his vicious vendetta against a female theologian. Unable to brush aside his comments, I took them personally and questioned both my work and myself.

Then a district leader in that denomination came to my defense, wrote to the reviewer, and then, receiving no repentance, publicly displayed in print the falsity of the original review. I was vindicated. Indeed, the valley of discouragement I'd been in was quickly lifted up.

An enormous geographical lifting and clearing is proclaimed in Isaiah 40:4, but possibly we have heard these words too often (in Handel's *Messiah* perhaps) to be startled by its imagery. What can be the purpose of lifting up the valleys and bringing down the high places? Following the command to prepare the highway for our God in verse 3, this verse asks for some tricky engineering. Why does faith have to move mountains anyway?

We need a geography lesson to answer these questions. If we regard the topography that Isaiah 40 describes as its first listeners understood it, we begin to comprehend the voice's message to them as well as to us, but we must look beneath the pictures of the land to see the powerful theology that underlies them. The voice is calling us to continue preparing by clearing out the obstructions that prevent God's coming. Two distinct operations are pictured in verse 4, each one accentuated by a poetic parallel.

The first two lines of the verse announce the lifting up of the low places and the bringing down of the high places. The first verb is very graphic; it actually shows the valleys coming up out of themselves, being pushed up to a position of exaltation. The same verb is used negatively in Ruth 1:9 to describe Naomi's daughters-in-law lifting up their voices in weeping over the agony of separation. We all know from experience the way such cries are forced up and out of us into uncontrollable sobs and wails.

The phrase here in Isaiah 40 is an indirect rebuke of the Hebrew people, who had pushed down the lowly by acts of injustice and oppression. (See the direct rebuke in Isaiah 3:9-26.) Thus, this phrase is not a romantic idyll — simply a lifting of Israel's discouragement in captivity — but a reminder that a removal of all oppressions is necessary to maintain Israel's own freedom from tyranny. God comes as the great equalizer.

22

While the valleys are being lifted, the mountains and high places are being brought down. The Hebrew word used here to designate those "high places" is used elsewhere in the First Testament to name the location of the altars at which the Israelites worshiped false gods. This declaration that the high places shall be made low rebukes Israel for its idolatries and reminds the people that a highway for God will be prepared only when all hilltop sanctuaries for idol worship are destroyed.

These phrases about valleys being lifted up and mountains brought low remind us of the words of Mary's Magnificat as she spoke of the poor being exalted and the rich being sent away empty (Luke 1:52-53). God does not tolerate our elevation of Mammon as the shrine at which we kneel.

The gulf between rich and poor in the United States and in the world keeps getting wider, and we can easily recognize that the tools of the information superhighway will continue to deepen the chasm. We could begin to reverse this trend only if we paid teachers in ghetto schools more than we do sports heroes.

What other kinds of oppressions are engaged in, for example, from both sides of the "political correctness" wars? What idolatries prevail in the business world and in academia that lead us to fanatic self-seeking and a deified sense of superiority? Against our tyrannies and god-making this verse speaks powerfully of a whole new order.

We experience God's new order already when we let the freedom of the gospel prevail, when we prepare to receive the LORD more thoroughly into our daily lives, and as we look to the day when Jesus will come again. In that freedom we no longer need to elevate ourselves or prove our worthiness. Instead, we have a unique opportunity as God's people to usher in the truth of the genuine equality and nobility that lie in God's choice of us to be his own.

What might be our task, then, in response to the voice

that is heard making this proclamation? Perhaps we can find practical ways to lift up those engulfed in sorrow or those swallowed by poverty. Perhaps we can serve as prophets to warn those who have elevated themselves to positions on economic or academic mountains or those engaged in worship of various other idolatries in high places. Whether we serve as compassionate priests or as rebuking prophets, our goal is to prepare the way for God to come more deeply into our own life and the lives of others.

Those who are sunk in the valleys, where they are convinced of their worthlessness, are not in any position to hear and receive the acceptance and love of God. It is true, to be sure, that God's acceptance of them will lift them up from their valleys, but those overwhelmed by their sin or grief or a situation of oppression need physical or emotional release from those tyrannies in order to receive God's grace thoroughly.

On the other hand, those puffed up with confidence in themselves, elevated on the mountains, need to be brought to recognize their fallibility before the perfection of the holy God. They need to recognize the idolatry of their worship of self if they think they have reached the high places of power or prestige.

Not only does all of this apply to our relationships with other people in our ministry to them, but it also offers tremendous resources for us personally. In our times of discouragement, we can believe the promise that we shall indeed be lifted up. On the other hand, in times of pride or self-satisfaction, when we lose sight of the fact that God is the one who accomplishes all things through us, we need God's rebuke (perhaps through the community or through this book) to be brought low. In both cases, the way of the LORD needs to be prepared so our lives will follow it.

The second set of two phrases in this verse speaks of openness and leveling, with the implication perhaps of productivity. The steep, hilly ground (translated as "uneven") named at

24

the beginning of the third line in verse 4 might indicate a rugged mountain path difficult to transcend. Places so characterized will become, the voice cries, as the *mishor,* which is a geographical term used in the Scriptures for two distinct places. It could mean either the Philistine plain around Gath and Gaza (the flat tableland west of Hebron) or the tableland east of the Dead Sea and south of the city of Amman. In both cases, the open plain is a profound contrast to that which is inaccessible. Consequently, the term *mishor* is used in the Scriptures figuratively to signify safety, comfort, and prosperity.

The poetic parallel of the last phrase in verse 4 asserts that the rugged terrain, which is impassable, shall become the *bukeah,* which is a little valley in the Judean wilderness on the north edge of the Dead Sea. Archaeological excavations in this area have shown that in the time of Uzziah (in the year of whose death Isaiah was called to be a prophet — see Isaiah 6) the *bukeah* was developed into a farming, military settlement. The rocks of the land were cleared and used to channel the moisture down from the hillsides above the fields and to dam the edges of the fields so that, in the midst of a relatively dry area, the *bukeah* became a series of terraced fields outlined in stones. In other words, the rough places will become garden spots.

This last set of poetic parallels implies, then, that the land that was untillable becomes usable. Consequently, this second half of verse 4 reminds me of Jesus' parable of the sowing of the seeds, in which those that fall into the good ground produce thirty, sixty, even a hundredfold (Mark 4:1-20). Soon verse 5 will declare that the glory of *YHWH* will be revealed. These phrases suggest that, as the ground of our will is prepared, it is made ready to be productive and fertile to bear that glory. The LORD uses the very stones of our lives to channel water for growth.

Again, this has implications both for our ministries and for our own lives. Perhaps our role is to eliminate distorted understandings of God so that others' minds are made accessible to God's planting. Perhaps we have to help tear away the obstructions of overcrowded schedules or to remove the rocks of vocational ambitions that prohibit lush growth — in ourselves or in others. Our personal need might be to channel God's ever-flowing waters through devotional disciplines to water our thirsty souls.

I am grateful for the caring of the board members of Christians Equipped for Ministry (under which I freelance), who knock off some of the rocky edges by constructively criticizing me when I lose track of ministry goals. I need their rebukes and continue to rely on their challenges to change.

The promise of the voice is that the rugged in us will become as the *mishor,* and the rough places will become as the *bukeah.* Our mountainous idolatries shall be brought down, and those who are victims of injustice shall be exalted.

After the geography lesson, now we need the bulldozers. We each have a lot of earth to move — and so do our churches.

QUESTIONS FOR FURTHER MEDITATION:

1. How have I been caught in valleys of oppression? How have I helped to put others there?

2. What does God use to lift me up from my valleys?

3. How can I be a means for lifting others up?

4. What does God use to bring me down from my idolatrous high places?

5. How can I be a constructive and gentle prophet in urging others to come down from pretentious heights?

6. How can I cultivate rough places to be more fertile, both in myself and in others in my Christian community?

7. How can I contribute to straightening some of the confusion and distortion of contemporary theological controversy?

5 The Cry of God's Revelation

"Then the glory of the LORD will be revealed,
and all flesh will see [it] together,
for the mouth of the LORD has spoken."

Isaiah 40:5 (NAS)

First we were too high, and the clouds below our plane hid it from sight. Much later, after we'd landed, the clouds above blocked it from view. Even when we were at the right level, I couldn't see it for a while — the plane's wings were in the way. But finally all obstructions were cleared away, and there it was: Mount Rainier towering majestically in all its snowy glory. It was an astonishingly beautiful sight, never in all these years forgotten. My ecstasy at the first moment of seeing it was heightened by the time of waiting and preparation. I anticipated a sublime vision of my favorite mountain in all the world, and I was not disappointed.

Similarly, we are filled with anticipation as we undertake the preparations described in the previous verses of Isaiah 40. Will what we see be worth its price? What will be the result in our lives when our valleys are lifted up, our heights brought low, our rough ground made fertile? The result, the voice proclaims, is that the glory of the LORD shall be revealed, and all people shall see it together.

When the book of Isaiah recorded the voice's message, it spoke of the reestablishment of the temple and the restoration of the people of Israel after their captivity in Babylon. The LORD's glory would be seen again in the promised land and, specifically, in God's dwelling place, the temple.

Then, in the history of Jesus, this cry was again fulfilled. Jesus himself was the new temple, and he revealed God's glory in the signs he performed and as he took up residence in the lives of God's people. This verse anticipates the revealing of the glory of the LORD on the mount of transfiguration and at the empty tomb. It prophesies such revealing of the LORD's glory as took place on Pentecost when all the people in Jerusalem saw it together. But what might this verse say to our lives now?

Several aspects of the original Hebrew text make the verse come alive for our times. The word *kabod,* which is translated "glory," means in its root "to be heavy," or "to make something important" or "weighty." Thus, the revealing of the glory of *YHWH* takes place when his importance is recognized, when his significant presence is made more fully known. Furthermore, that glorious revealing will be all the greater, verse 5 goes on to say, because all flesh shall see it together as one. I am disappointed that the New Revised Standard Version limits its translation to "people," because the Hebrew word for "flesh" can also signify animals. The phrase indicates that certainly all people will see it, no doubt about it, but perhaps also all creatures are designated. God's revelation of himself will be unmistakable.

The inevitability of that revelation is reinforced by the assertion, "For the mouth of the LORD has spoken." Both the noun phrase and the verb form are made more intensive by their construction in the original Hebrew. Consequently, they declare in no uncertain terms that *YHWH* himself has promised this revelation of his glory. And we know, for God has never failed yet, that his promise will be fulfilled. The entire narrative of the First and Second Testaments, the Scriptures of the Jews and the Christians, demonstrates that God's promises are always fulfilled.

How is God's promise to be fulfilled for us in our time? Ultimately, this verse looks forward to the day when Jesus will return in full glory, and, as Philippians 2:10-11 confirms, the whole world will see his glory together. Every knee shall bow, and every tongue shall confess Jesus as Lord, to the glory of God the Father. We know this will occur, for the mouth of the LORD has spoken — and when the LORD speaks, it is done.

This last phrase of verse 5 is a tremendous climax to the message the voice declares, for everything is sealed by the fact that the message originates with God. There need not be any doubt, for when God has declared something, it has always and will surely come to pass. Indeed, this verse asserts the sovereignty of God, his majestic omnipotence, his unalterable ability to fulfill that which he announces.

God especially wants to fulfill this verse through us. The apostle Paul highlights this idea in 2 Corinthians 3:18, where he declares that, as we behold the glory of the Lord, we shall be changed into his likeness, from one degree of glory to another. The glory of the LORD shall indeed be revealed *in our lives* in ways that are observable.

God's glory is so multifaceted (an image in 1 Peter 4:10) that it requires all of us individuals to reveal all that God wants to say to us about himself. Consequently, Christians are to be neither nonentities nor carbon copies of each other, but unique vessels for God's self-revelation. We are each matchlessly created in God's image and have much to reveal to the world around us. If the wildernesses of our lives can be properly prepared — with valleys lifted, mountains brought low, unevennesses smoothed — then God's glory can shine through observably.

Now, lest any of us get discouraged thinking we are failures because our lives don't reveal God's glory as they should, we must quickly be reminded that God is the one who does the revealing. Not by our own efforts does his glory shine through us. Not by our own abilities can we be the particular people God created us to be. In and of ourselves we are incapable of revealing God's glory — often because we strive instead to reveal our own glory and discover that there is nothing there. In fact, as Paul asserts in 2 Corinthians 4:7 and 12:9, the fact that we are but clay vessels, our very weaknesses, best reveal God's glory, for our weaknesses make it obvious that the transcendent power belongs to him. The possibility of revealing God's glory, then, is another gift of grace, which enters our lives to transform us into the image of God.

This promise is made real in our lives as we heed the voice crying out for us to prepare in the wilderness the way of the LORD. As our lives become more and more attuned to the will of God, as we seek him, not just to know *about* him, but to *know him,* his glory shall be revealed in us.

This verse is part of a strong scriptural theme that begins with the time of the tabernacle in the wilderness. Exodus 40 gives us the stunning narration of the filling of the tabernacle with the glorious presence of God himself. As his glory is revealed, God pitches the tent of his presence — he "tabernacles" himself — among the Israelites.

In John 1:14, this same imagery is uniquely employed when the evangelist declares, "the Word became flesh and tabernacled himself among us." The sentence testifies in a very vivid way that God became human in the person of Jesus, who literally "pitched his tent" among human beings by coming to earth.

The same Greek verb, meaning "to pitch one's tent," is used in Revelation 21:3, where we read the glorious promise that the dwelling of God shall be with his people, for he shall at the end of time "tabernacle himself among us." Again, the apostle

Paul uses the same verb in 2 Corinthians 12:9 when he asserts that he glories in his weaknesses, for in them he experiences the "tabernacling" of God. It is in our weakness, especially, that God can pitch his tent in our lives to reveal his glory.

When we repentantly acknowledge our miserable failures, our arrogant presumptions, our mistaken efforts, our misdirected abilities, our self-centered ambitions, and our subtle idolatries, then God's power at work *on* us can be brought to its finish. Then his glory can be revealed *through* us, and the world around us will see it. The mouth of *YHWH* has spoken, and he will do it. The LORD wants to work that kind of transformation in our lives. Are we ready to receive it?

All of this has tremendous implications for the Church in our postmodern times. The weakness of our churches and the lack of impact by Christianity in our culture could be overcome if all believers yearned to reveal God's glory in their lives. Do our worship services stir us up to be eager to carry God's glory into our world? Is the relationship to God of many of our congregation's members confined to hours of worship and minutes of pious prayer, or do we remember that the LORD wants to come mightily into and through every moment of our lives?

The challenge before Christians is not what we do for the LORD, but who we are by his fashioning. He wants to conform us to his image, to bring us down and lift us up, to straighten us out and remove our obstructions, so that his glory can be revealed in us and through us, from one degree to another.

QUESTIONS FOR FURTHER MEDITATION:

1. *In what ways does God reveal his glory to me?*
2. *What other places in the Scriptures speak about the* LORD's *glory being revealed?*

31

3. How have I been an instrument for revealing God's glory to others?

4. How can I encourage others to look for God's revelation of himself?

5. Where else in the Scriptures is it declared that God will accomplish everything he has asserted?

6. How does the fact that God's glory will surely be finally and fully revealed when Jesus returns affect my day-to-day existence?

7. What are the implications of this verse for my church — in the larger denomination to which we belong and as an individual assembly of believers?

6 *The Cry of Human Sehnsucht*

A voice says, "Cry out!"
  And I said, "What shall I cry?"
All [flesh is] grass,
  their constancy is like the flower of the field.

Isaiah 40:6

Chesed
    steadfast love

I had thought my apartment upkeep days were over. I moved into a brand-new house when I first came to the West Coast, and I thought that at last I was free for a few years from the bother of old things wearing out. But I had falsely assumed that everyone built things as durably as did my grandfather. Doesn't everybody strive after excellence? How naive I was to think that things are still made to last. I was shocked by the poorly constructed cabinets and dismayed that the stud nails showed through the white paint. The exterior of the house needed to be repainted within its first three years. What has happened to the ideals of quality and permanence? Surely you, too, have been exasperated by slipshod labor and the lack of attention to work that lasts.

And don't we all hate the merciless onrush of time? None

of us has enough opportunity for everything we'd like to do along with everything we must do. Even as a child, I hated how fast time sped by — moments that I craved for reading and swimming, playing baseball and chasing fireflies. Time passes away as fast as the roses. Life grows and goes as quickly as the grass.

Exactly! The New Revised Standard Version once again translates the first noun in line 3 as "people," but the Hebrew word is better rendered "flesh" so that we see a progression from all flesh seeing God's glory together in verse 5 to the personalness of "people" in verse 7. All flesh like grass, its constancy like field flowers — our human recognition of the transience of life echoes this declaration by an eternal God. The glaring question is what to do about it.

The prophet again hears the voice — this time calling to him to cry out. When he responds, "What is it that I should proclaim?" he is told to announce the evanescence of human life. The Israelites experienced that impermanence when their pride was shattered and their glorious temple destroyed in their defeat by the Babylonians. They discovered that their power was fleeting, their place among the nations short-lived. This prophetic message pertained painfully to that particular moment in their history.

So it also applies particularly to our history. Not only are we distressingly aware of our momentary existence because we live in an age of planned obsolescence, but we also behold the rapid changes in political clout, the tragedies befalling world leaders thrust from power, the swift destructions of earthquakes, civil wars, and famines. Ephemerality surrounds us, but how often do we face the fact as applied directly to us? YOUR flesh is grass; MY constancy is like the flower of the field.

The comparison is so strong that it requires no word such as *like* or *as* and not even a verb in the Hebrew. All flesh, grass. Just as God IS eternal, all flesh IS short-lived. Our durability, furthermore, is like that of a field flower — fading quickly, perhaps without ever being noticed. The Hebrew word translated "constancy" is *chesedh*, more often rendered "loving kindness" or "steadfast love." This noun is used in all the descriptions of God's mercy, which is dependable, unchangeable, fresh every morning in its faithfulness. While his goodness is sure and true, to be counted upon, ours is as the daylilies, quickly passing away. Even our attempts to be good are incomplete and unstable. So the voice urges the prophet and us to proclaim this sorely needed message to our times: We are to remind our society, our churches, and ourselves that nothing lasts.

Too often in our personal lives we forget this truth and mindlessly invest all our time, all our energies, all our resources, and all our care in things that will only pass away. We spend our work gaining wealth, our effort building power, our talents achieving fame, our love comforting ourselves — only to discover in the end that these things, too, will fade and in the meanwhile will not satisfy our deepest longings.

C. S. Lewis, in his insightful theory of *Sehnsucht* (discussed in his autobiography, *Surprised by Joy*, and elsewhere), made clear for me the nature of human longing. He used the German term *Sehnsucht* to describe our desire for fulfillment that nothing seems to satisfy more than temporarily. He recognized that *Sehnsucht* results from our being made in the image of God, and every person has it. All the people I've discussed that idea with, both Christians and non-Christians, have admitted that such an insatiable longing or intense yearning does indeed exist deep within them.

Lewis proposed that there are three ways in which this *Sehnsucht* is handled. The first is the "fool's way." The fool thinks that if she can reach a particular goal, she will be satisfied. Consequently, she struggles and strives to achieve that goal, only to discover in the end, having reached the goal, that it cannot satisfy her for long. The result is that she spends her life jumping from one inadequate goal to another.

35

The second way to handle *Sehnsucht* is the "sensible person's way." This "wise person" recognizes that his longing deep inside cannot be stilled, so he tries instead to push it under. This, too, is unsuccessful, however, for the longing keeps surfacing, and the attempts to push it under — by means of alcohol, drugs, sex, partying, or even religious piety — must continually be redoubled to keep the lid on the growing tension and anxiety.

The third way to deal with *Sehnsucht*, Lewis suggests, is the only way truly to handle the nature of the longing itself. We can come to realize that if we have such an intense longing and (#1) nothing in the world satisfies it, and (#2) nothing in the world can push it under, then (#3) we must be made for another world.

The reason that the fool's way cannot work is found in these words from Isaiah 40:6: "All flesh is grass, and its constancy like the flower of the field." Nothing in this world will ever satisfy our deepest longings, because everything in this world is merely temporary. We look around at all the things on which we stake our happiness and discover that they all provide only fleeting satisfaction.

Don't we all experience frustration that even our happiest moments are marred by their transience? We cannot hold on to them. Every vacation with relatives from far away is affected by the unwelcome awareness that our time together is so terribly short. The gorgeous flowers that bedeck our lawn will droop soon; even the magnificent beauty of Mount Saint Helens was stripped in one cataclysmic volcanic explosion. All earthly sources of happiness will, at some point before or at death, pass away.

This is the message we have to cry. It is a declaration indispensable in our times, when the "fool's way" of striving after fulfillment is so dominant. It seems, however, to be such an utterance of despair. How can we handle such a burdensome word, this realization that all flesh is grass? Two verses later we will find the most important answer to that problem, but meanwhile we can consider from C. S. Lewis's perspective a simple fact that will enable us to cope with the burden of this prophetic pronouncement.

To realize fully that our flesh is grass will not lead us to despair unless we are dependent upon our own flesh for fulfillment, unless we don't have our priorities straight. The good news of our faith in Christ is that we are not in the slightest dependent upon these ephemeral things. The third way to handle our *Sehnsucht* is profoundly true; we are indeed "made for another world."

The good news of Jesus Christ is that he has overcome the ephemerality of grass and field flowers. In fact, he uses those same elements to illustrate the basis for our hope. In Matthew 6:28 Jesus says, "Consider the lilies of the field," and tells us to look at their beauty and glory. Even Solomon in all his glory was not arrayed as they are, and yet, Jesus says, they pass away. If our Father invested such care in clothing them with beauty, however, certainly we can trust him to take care of us, too.

The fact that our flesh is fleeting should do this one thing: It should drive us to total dependence upon the one who does not pass away. That is the conclusion Lewis reached with such a stroke of genius. If the things of the world do not ultimately satisfy, if they do not push under our deepest longings, we can come to the realization that we are indeed made for another world — and that that world has already entered our own and changed it eternally.

QUESTIONS FOR FURTHER MEDITATION:

 1. How does my world try to hide the fact that it is temporary?
 2. How do I hide that fact from myself?
 3. What are some of the goals I have set for myself, thinking that if I achieved them I would be satisfied?

4. What means do I use to try to push under my discontentment?

5. What has happened as I have used these means to try to still the Sehnsucht *deep within me?*

6. How have I experienced the satisfaction of realizing that I am made for another world?

7. How might the Church better cry out to the world this message of its ephemerality?

7 *Our Cry of Transience*

The grass withers, the flower fades,
  when the breath of the LORD blows upon it;
  surely the people are grass.

Isaiah 40:7

The editor of the campus newspaper sat in my office and told me why he chose to be a "militant atheist." "Why is there so much evil in the world if your God hasn't sent it?" My responses did not successfully convince him that God is not the creator of destruction.

"God is cruel, and I just can't believe in a God who willfully hurts people." Probably you have also heard that argument from postmodernists who insist that the biblical God and the narratives of Scripture are oppressive. This seventh verse from Isaiah 40 seems at first glance to add ammunition to their attacks, for it appears to suggest that flesh withers and loveliness fades *because* the LORD sends his destructive breath upon them. How can biblically formed people answer that objection?

The argument against God seems to be fortified even more

when we look at the literal original Hebrew of this verse. "Withers, green grass" — the same verb root is found in Genesis 1:10 when the dry land separated from the water appears on the earth by God's command. "Droops, a blossom" — the noun form of this verb signifies a corpse. Both of these symptoms occur when the breath, or spirit, of *YHWH* passes over them. Who needs a God seemingly so destructive?

However, the key to understanding lies in realizing that these events are indeed *symptoms*. Fading occurs when the LORD's breath passes over the flowers because of their nature, which existed *prior* to its coming. The withering demonstrates that flesh is grass in the first place, as the end of this verse reaffirms. "Surely" — the poetic device cries out, "Yes, indeed!" — "green grass, the people."

The pronouncement therefore concerns the glaring contrast between God's power and righteousness and the weakness of human beings. The picture is not the image of people mowed down like grass, complete victims when God arbitrarily blows over them — and suddenly they are gone. Rather, the verse presents an honest realization of human destiny, of what we genuinely deserve.

This difficult truth was clarified for me by a movie called *The Antkeeper,* which our regional youth board used several times for training sessions more than twenty years ago. In this film, God is represented by a gardener, and human beings are pictured as two flying ants. Shortly after the movie's beginning, the ants fly to a section of the flora to which the gardener had forbidden them to go — a graphic representation of the fall of human beings into sin, of our profound propensity to choose our own way. Having flown to that prohibited plot, they alight on an insect-devouring plant, which immediately closes and traps them inside. As the two ants struggle to be free, their buzzing is heard by the gardener, who stands, conversing with his son, far off on the other side of the hilltop.

With majestic stateliness and restrained anger, he slowly walks to the plant. Throughout his march, the cameras offer panoramic views of the garden — all the lovely places to which the ants could freely have gone — and then return to the gardener's face to capture his righteous indignation. He had warned those ants for their own good. When he arrives at the closed plant with the ants buzzing frantically inside, he grasps it firmly in his hand and holds it for a prolonged moment.

Although I saw that movie several times, each time, during that excruciatingly long moment, I experienced deep tension. For a split second that lasts an eternity, it seems that the gardener will crush the plant in his stern grasp. As he held it in his hand, I knew with a shudder that to be annihilated is what the ants deserve. It always seemed to me in that terrible moment that the gardener *should* express his righteous outrage by destroying those ants.

But he does not obliterate them. Instead, he opens the plant very carefully, draws the ants out into his hand, and removes their wings. Eventually, his own son becomes an ant and enters their valley to save them from their self-destruction.

Although this small moment is not one of the major scenes in the movie, it has continued to stand out in my mind most vividly. Each time, at that point — and now as I rewrite this book many years later — I have understood more clearly the scriptural tension of fear and love in our relationship with God.

Too frequently in our postmodern, tolerant world we lose sight of that tension, although it is often described in the Scriptures. For example, many of the Psalms speak of both the profound fear with which the poets have observed the fact of death or God's actions in nature and the love with which they adore their covenant God. Similarly, the apostle Paul agonizes over his bondage to sin (Romans 7) just before exulting over the Truth that nothing can separate us from the love of God (Romans 8).

41

We can hardly begin to know the amazing grace of God's love unless we first have known how much we deserve his righteous wrath, how much we deserve the death we each must die. Otherwise, we assume that it's easy for God to forgive us. We think that we're not too bad — that we can actually earn God's favor. We make grace cheap. When we totally confront our absolute hopelessness and complete depravity, however, we recognize with awe the majesty and infinity and incomprehensibility of God's love for us. God could at any moment destroy us; that is what we deserve. But he does not; that is his grace.

"The grass withers, the flower fades, when the breath of the LORD blows upon it." Readers of this verse in biblical times probably thought immediately of the sirocco, the wind that comes off the Arabian desert. Residents around Jerusalem knew, and still know, how in just a few short moments the lush spring grasses of southern Palestine are quickly destroyed when it blows. That is the inherent power of God made visible in an earthly analogy.

In the context of all of Isaiah 40, however, we realize that God does not arbitrarily vent his power upon people. His wind does not blow by chance, for his steadfast love (*chesedh,* see Chapter 6), in contrast to ours, is faithful. He comes to us with grace.

When we recognize his sovereign but restrained power, our love for our gracious Father in heaven is deepened. Because we know we deserve to be squashed, like the flying ants trapped because of their bad choices, our adoration and thanksgiving are so much greater, our purpose and meaning so much deeper. Jesus speaks of this fact when the Pharisees criticize the woman who had anointed him (Luke 7:36-50). How much more thankful she is, he asserts, because she knows how precious it is to be forgiven!

Isaiah 40:7 concludes, "Surely the people are grass." Now for the first time the text moves specifically to people. Surely we deserve the wrath of God because we are totally incapable of loving God perfectly and living out of that love. People are no more enduring than other flesh — beasts and plants. If we base our hopes upon our own ability to create our life, we are surely going to be crushingly disappointed. We who cannot endure will inevitably fail. If we genuinely face ourselves, with the help of this verse, we have to admit that we are not able to change our fragile natures. It is not possible for us to make ourselves capable of avoiding the fate we deserve.

U.S. society at the turn of the century does everything it can to euphemize or avoid death, even though the ratio is always the same: one per person. The present mushrooming of the euthanasia movement and its attempt to glorify death is a sad commentary on our culture's vapid misunderstanding of suffering and death and of the preeminence of death and emptiness in its life. Without doubt we cannot miss the truth of this analogy that we are like the grass. The voice says, "Cry," and we are told to cry out about our fate.

The biblical narratives make clear that death is God's gift to us — to keep us from having to live forever in this sin-broken and rebelliously corrupted world. Death is the door into meeting God face to face. What will we find on the other side of the door? To be biblically formed is to be prepared for that encounter in the present recognition of God's powerful breath and our withering nature, of God's cosmic transcendence and our puny ephemerality.

Our Joy and wonder in God's resurrecting love are deepened if we thoroughly understand that surely we are grass. In the community of God's people, our worship teaches us the necessary awe; in the texts of Scripture, the message is continually proclaimed. In one of the Church's ancient prayers, used at funerals, this phrase suggests our response to the intent of verse 7: "Teach us all so to number our days that we may apply our hearts unto wisdom and finally be saved." We know the power of *YHWH*; he is LORD of life and death. We know the frailty of human beings; surely the people are grass. These two facts together call us to

43

number our days. Realizing who we are and who God is, we can apply our hearts unto wisdom, not trust ourselves for any type of salvation, and rejoice in the one whose breath also creates life.

QUESTIONS FOR FURTHER MEDITATION:

1. What circumstances or events help me become more conscious of my transience?

2. Martin Luther spoke about dire despair as a prerequisite for truly knowing the love of God. What have been some times in my life when recognizing how much I deserved God's wrath has deepened my awareness of his infinite love?

3. What biblical passages teach me about the tension between fear and love?

4. What are the results of an overemphasis on one side or the other in the dialectical tension of fear and love?

5. At what stages in the history of Christianity has one side or the other been overemphasized, and what were the results?

6. How can I keep both sides in their proper perspective and balance?

7. How might my understanding of this verse be a tool for presenting the truth of Christianity to my neighbors who doubt its importance?

8 *The Cry of God's Absolutivity*

The grass withers, the flower fades;
but the word of our God will stand forever.

Isaiah 40:8

I never liked the anthem until its ending. When our college choir went around the world on a mission concert tour, we sang a setting of Acts 2 that was full of discordant notes until almost the very last chord. At times we all spoke the lines of the crowd — each at our own tempo. The message of the piece was powerful, but the chaos and discordancy sometimes seemed too unnerving —

Until we reached the song's conclusion, and the entire musical structure changed. The chords the choir sang melted into a lovely resolution on the final words of the text, "but whoever calls on the name of the Lord shall be saved." The symmetry of the sound, the climax of the content, the focus finally reached gave us all a profound sense of peace.

The eighth verse of Isaiah 40 presents an equally dramatic resolution. After two verses of negative assertions about withering and fading, verse 8 moves beyond those statements to the hope of something positive. There is something enduring, something to which we can cling. The Word of our God stands forever. It alone will not evaporate in time.

An understanding of Hebrew poetic forms helps us to see the tremendous drama of this verse. The basic element in First Testament poetry is the set of two *synonymous* parallel lines in which the corresponding clause pieces state essentially the same thing. This parallelism is sometimes extended by the addition of an extra phrase to the second line so that the couplet becomes *climactic,* or stairlike. The parallelism is at other times inverted or made *antithetical,* in which case the second line says the opposite of the first.

In Isaiah 40:6-8, the prophet constructs a tremendous sequence of exquisite poetry, building to an overwhelming conclusion with a sudden antithesis. The first phrase, "All flesh is grass," is paralleled by "its constancy is like the flower of the field." We might represent these lines by a^1 and a^2. Next, "the grass withers" is paralleled by "the flower fades." These are represented by b^1 and b^2. Then the second line (b^2) is expanded with "when the breath of the LORD blows upon it," which we will call c. Then the text returns to a^1 when, for emphasis, the prophet declares, "Surely the people are grass." Finally, in verse 8, b^1 and b^2 are repeated in "The grass withers, the flower fades," and then abruptly, dramatically, these are opposed by NOT B: "The word of our God stands forever."

Swiftly across our vision sweeps the opposite of all the voice has been saying, and we are astounded. This arresting decree is as startling as Georgia O'Keefe's shocking pink rose painted in the midst of a dreary scene of dull browns and rainy grays, or a trumpet fanfare in the midst of hushed flutes and soft strings. The progression looks like this:

a^1 a^2
b^1 b^2c
a^1
b^1 b^2
NOT B

Immediately we want to know more deeply the truth of this NOT B. What does this brilliant shaft of light mean? How or in what way does the Word of God stand forever? How can we be sure that the Word of God does not fade or wither? Can we really stake our life on the assertion that it shall indeed stand forever?

An emphasis on *YHWH's* Word, of course, pervades the Scriptures. In the First Testament, it is by the Word of his mouth that God creates. The Hebrew verb *dabar* (to speak) is so certain — that is, what the LORD speaks will come to pass — that the noun derived from it in time came to mean "event." In the Second Testament, it is the Word himself, Jesus the Christ, who becomes incarnated to "tabernacle" among us (John 1:14). God is a promising God, who never breaks his promises. In our post-modern world, which doubts the possibility of an overarching story, God's Word provides a metanarrative — personalized in the incarnate Word — of God's love and care throughout time and space. Jesus Christ fulfilled all the prophetic words about him, especially that he would rise from the dead. The fact of Easter enables us to know that God's Word does indeed abide forever. Christ incarnated God's Word in time and continues to fulfill it for and in us as he takes up residence in our lives. What might this mean practically?

First, and probably most important, we can't help but recognize the stability and security that the steadfastness of God's Word provides. "When every earthly prop gives way," the old hymn asserts, "He then is all my Hope and Stay. / On Christ the solid Rock

I stand; / all other ground is sinking sand." God's Word to us in the person of Jesus the Christ is a reference point, a source of equilibrium, a message of grace, the promise of forgiveness and healing that stands forever, in spite of our failures and sin and brokenness. God's Word to us is Love, even though we are unlovable or unloved by the world around us. God's Word to us is Joy in the midst of sorrow and pain, Peace in the midst of tension and anxiety, Hope in the face of insurmountable obstacles and death. This is the basis of our faith: the realization that God's Word of victory over the powers of evil and of freedom from sin and death is true and eternal. Who can describe the ecstasy that such a Word creates?

Second, this assertion has powerful implications for the way we minister to other people. Why give them fading fantasies or withering words when instead we could communicate to them the sure hope and promises of an eternal Word? This was emphasized in Chapter 1 when we considered the possibility of deep and meaningful comfort in the face of tragedy. Why do we try to comfort others out of our own resources when we have all the sure promises of heaven at our fingertips?

Human words can't guarantee their fulfillment. When we offer our merely human words to comfort, we forget that all flesh is grass. That merely human words are often empty gifts is amply demonstrated by the overinflated campaign promises of political candidates or the overblown claims of television advertising. But even persons who love us deeply can't always keep their promises or live by their claims, since the tragedies of life can preclude their best intentions.

In contrast, the eternal Word of God carries inherently within it the power to accomplish what it describes. If we say to someone, "Grace and peace to you from God . . . ," those words carry within them the actual fact of grace and peace, already bequeathed in the Word of Christ, really to be received by our listener.

Why does God's Word prove to be genuine, meaningful, substantive, and eternal? It is all these things and more because Jesus the Word does not merely point to the truth; he IS the Truth, and his written Word conveys his presence. He is there, incarnated in his Word to bring it about. The Word was made flesh to tabernacle among us, a historic fact absolutely too glorious to grasp with only our rational minds.

The tremendous applicability of these words to our increasingly postmodern and mixed-up times stirs us; we want zealously to follow the instructions of the voice that says, "Cry!" People are longing for some sort of Truth, some kind of reference point by which to sort out their lives and find meaning. Our postmodern society craves substance and confidence. How powerfully this message could benefit our searching neighbors if we could show them more grace-fully their own fallibility in light of the eternal immutability of the Word of God.

In Chaim Potok's novel *My Name Is Asher Lev,* a famous painter defines whether or not one is an artist by "whether or not there is a scream in him wanting to get out in a special way." His friend then immediately adds, "Or a laugh." Pondering that bit of dialogue, I realize with repentance and with rapture that Christians have both. God's people know the scream, for it is painful to acknowledge that all flesh is grass and to live in its withered failures. We weep with the world's sorrows of brokenness and faded dreams.

But Christians also can't help but laugh. We laugh with victory over despair. We laugh eternally. We bubble with delight because we are God's children. We giggle in the freedom of divine approval. The promise stands forever that grace is the foundation of the world and undergirds our lives. God's eternal Word assures us of eternal life with him — already begun.

Recognizing that it is a privilege to proffer this double-sided message, the artist's scream and laugh, gave rise to this book nearly twenty years ago, and I find it even more important now.

How desperately our culture waits for us to respond to that voice which says, "Cry!" You and I can carry eternal truths away from our devotional time and into our world today. How will the Word of God go with us into our daily situations?

What promise and hope this verse gives us to pass on to those around us. When accomplishments fall apart or fade away, we remember God's steadfast Word of grace. When our neighbors look for something deeper than the world's shallow and content-less entertainments, we can offer the substance of God's purposes and eternal meanings for our lives. In the frustrations of the workplace, we can offer an abiding hope that does not disappoint. When loved ones die, we grieve in the cry that flesh is grass, but we can also rejoice in the laugh of God's Word about resurrection. When feeble friends turn away or the empty promises of the world fail us, the scream of loneliness is contradicted by the laugh of Jesus, whose Word, "Surely I am with you always," stands forever.

In every situation of life we confront grass and fading flowers. This eighth verse of Isaiah 40 promises, however, that we can also find this laugh: The Word of the LORD abides forever! Our laughter passes the gift to others who also need to hear an abiding Word.

QUESTIONS FOR FURTHER MEDITATION:

1. *What other images could we use to describe the glorious contradiction between the ephemeral things of the world and the eternal steadfastness of God's Word?*

2. *At what times that I regret did I minister to other people with only superficial comfort?*

3. *How could I have given them an eternal and abiding Word instead?*

4. What have been some of the screams in the situations of my life in the last few days?

5. What have been the laughs?

6. What goals could I set for myself in order to get to know the eternal Word of God better?

7. What are some of the implications of this verse for the members of my congregation?

9 *The Cry for Heralding*

Get you up to a high mountain,
    O Zion, herald of good tidings;
lift up your voice with strength,
    O Jerusalem, herald of good tidings,
    lift it up, do not fear;
say to the cities of Judah,
    "Here is your God!"

Isaiah 40:9

Have you ever known anyone to mumble when announcing to her best friend that she has just become engaged? Of course not; she proclaims the news joyously. And have you heard the fans scream as they parade through the hometown streets after winning a league football championship? My high school peers would shout, "And if you can't hear us, we'll yell a little louder."

Love stories and sports pride and Isaiah 40:9 all illustrate the principles of heralding good news. "Get you up to a high mountain," Zion is told. "Lift up your voice with strength," Jerusalem is commanded. If you have good news to tell, make sure you are visible to all, and then say it again louder, to be sure it's heard.

I love the poetic repetition of this verse, with its thrilling emphasis on the privilege that is ours. We could modernize the prophet's reiteration in this way: "Broadcast it from the mountaintops, you people of God, couriers of the good news. Proclaim it in every way, you saints who are messengers of this good news. Shout still more; don't be afraid. Say to each and every one who dwells in your land, 'Look! Your God is here!'"

The prophet's words to Zion are especially urgent for us now. In this postmodern, post-Christian age, we all need this kind of pep-rally encouragement to stir us up. A mistaken view of pluralism makes us afraid to speak about our commitment, and we fail to realize the incredible hunger for the good news we have to proclaim. Look at this message we are to cry out: Our God is here! How can we be so unmoved by such good news? (Or do we perhaps not believe God is really here?)

How are we to cry out this information? The commands of verse 9 follow a deliberate progression. First we are told to declare the good news, not from the valleys or the churches, but boldly from the top of the mountains, out in the open. Both words from verse 4 are put together here to emphasize the high places of the mountaintops. We are to get ourselves up to those lofty peaks as pilgrims go up to the temple of *YHWH*.

We have allowed the society around us to chase us out of the public square. Our failures in the past, when we have told the story of the faith in oppressive ways, has scared us away from faithful heralding. I see people all around me — on airplanes, in my neighborhood, in the school where my husband teaches, in the grocery store — yearning for better news, for hope, for a point of reference by which to understand their lives. The word for "heralding" in this verse is an intensive participle; we are to proclaim our truth exuberantly.

53

Next, we are to exalt, or lift up, our voices with great strength. The word *strength* here anticipates its climactic use in verse 31, wherein those who wait upon the LORD find their strength renewed. Here this phrase accentuates extra effort; once we have gotten ourselves into a prominent place, we are to extend our voices even more to make sure the message is heard. This extra effort is again called for by the poetic stairstepping repetition of the verb "lift it up."

But wait. Perhaps what holds us back is our fear. The positive encouragement is suddenly interrupted, almost as if to say, "What's the matter? Is fear the problem behind your delay? Then cast it aside!" Immediately, then, this negative reprimand is swallowed up by the glorious content of our heralding, "Behold your God!" We are to introduce him to the cities of Judah, to the people nearby.

This geographical designation, spoken as it was to Zion/Jerusalem, connotes the neighbors. It is the first step in loving evangelism. We have the privilege of saying to our friends next door and down the block and in the next office, "Let me introduce you to God!"

Churches try so frantically to institute evangelism programs or evangelistic worship services (which is a confusion of adoring God and speaking to the neighbor, to the detriment of both[1]) and forget that our witness takes place within our daily lives, in ordinary interactions and loving relationships. The Greek text of the Great Commission literally says, "[While] going, be making disciples of all nations . . ." (Matthew 28:19).

Many evangelism programs are very well prepared and can be quite helpful for teaching people how to speak about God,

---

1. See Marva J. Dawn, *Reaching Out without Dumbing Down: A Theology of Worship for the Turn-of-the-Century Culture* (Grand Rapids: Wm. B. Eerdmans, 1995).

but faithful evangelism cannot be programmed. Our witness comes instead from a spontaneous reaction to the Joy-full realization that God is here and from a genuine love for the neighbor.

When was the last time you were extremely excited about something? Was it hard to tell someone else about it? Did you wring your hands in nervousness and stew and fret about whether you would have the right words? Chances are the words simply tumbled out in an enthusiastic burst. We can speak so easily about the good things that happen in our daily lives, yet, as the previous three verses reminded us, these very good things are only going to pass away. Now here we have a message that abides forever — our God is here! — and yet we are actually afraid to tell other people. We are afraid they might be offended, or we are bothered by the bad example of television preachers, worried about our inadequacies, too busy, perhaps too self-centered and preoccupied. One of the greatest needs of contemporary Christian churches is to recover the invitation of this verse for our times. We need the boldness of the Hebrew prophets, the exuberance of the early Christians, the contagion of brand-new Christians who cannot help but tell those around them that God is here.

Getting up to a high mountain or going where we can be seen doesn't mean we are to be ostentatious or flamboyant (and certainly not obnoxious) about our witness. We don't have to stand on a soapbox on the street corner. We're not encouraged by this verse to adopt marketing strategies or "show biz" techniques that give the gospel the ill-suited flavor of the hard-sell approach.

On the contrary, verse 9 means that our news is too good to keep quiet about or merely to mumble under our breath. We are encouraged, in our Joy over the presence of the LORD, to witness freely, openly, even if that might cause us to become a target for persecution (as long as we are persecuted for the sake of the gospel and not because we deserve it!). The nature of the good news about God's gracious care for us is such that we don't mind being seen; we find it a privilege to tell others about the One we see, especially because those down in the valley need to hear that a God who can lift them up is here.

In earlier cultures — Roman or Greek or Hebrew — when the bearer of good tidings, such as the news of victory in battle, got up to a high mountain to shout, he didn't have to worry about how he would be received. He knew that everybody was waiting for the message he had to give. Why do we fail to realize the immense goodness of our message? Why do we let the world set the agenda for our conversation with those we love? Why do we let our culture drive us to embarrassment about it? We don't have to be ashamed, Paul asserts (Romans 1:16), for our message is the power of God for salvation — in the largest sense of that word. Our eagerness to be heralds is a natural outflow of our being overwhelmed by the good news of the message. We don't have to be afraid to proclaim it; after all, those who would per-secute us are only grass. The Word we proclaim will bear itself out as Truth, as it continues to endure. Our task is simply to introduce those who listen to the fact that God is here.

Besides its application to our evangelism, this verse prods the Christian community to greater care for each other in the Body of Christ. Verse 9 commands us to lift our voices and not to fear as we remind other members, who might be down in valleys and having trouble seeing, that God is here. We can gently offer a different perspective and incarnate for them tangibly God's loving presence in our own hugs, listening ears, and tender, practical concern. The secret of building the Christian community is the privilege of taking others by the hand to reveal to them the presence of God. This is the center of the gospel. Without God we have nothing. If *YHWH* is here, behold: we have everything.

One final observation: What gives this verse its tre-mendous freedom is that we are called by the name *heralds of good tidings.* The person who serves as such an envoy is totally responsible only to the source of her message. She does not have to worry about the reaction to her words; it isn't her responsibility to convert or convince. Her only mission is to proclaim as faithfully as she can the wisdom she has been given with the character of its Giver.

We are called to be heralds. Though we will be as gentle and compassionate, as inviting and affirming as possible, we do not have to fear how our deeds of encouragement or our words of witness will be received. We are called only to report faithfully those good tidings that are ours to give: "Behold your God!" All we do is tell others that the LORD is here; the rest is up to God.

QUESTIONS FOR FURTHER MEDITATION:

1. Which people that I know specifically need to hear that God is here?

2. How can I gently and reverently (see 1 Peter 3:15-16) communicate to those people that God is here?

3. What kinds of fears keep me from telling others that God is here?

4. How can I become more aware in my own life of the fullness of God's presence?

5. What are the strong points of my congregation's evangelism program (if it has one) or its witness to the neighborhood?

6. What are the weaknesses of my congregation's witness, and what can I do about them?

7. How can I safeguard my own witness and that of my congregation from phoniness and superficiality?

10 *The Cry of YHWH's Might*

Behold, the Lord GOD comes with might,
  with His arm ruling for Him.
Behold, His reward is with Him
  and His recompense before Him.

Isaiah 40:10 (NAS)

The Olympic marathon gold medalist was captured by the newspaper snapshot in a victory pose with arm raised triumphantly and face beaming with excitement. There could be no doubt that she had been the strongest. Her victory celebration spread across the country. Like a journal photograph, Isaiah 40:10 invites us to behold the victory pose of the Lord GOD. He comes with might, his arm rules for him, and he brings along a victory celebration. The previous verse had announced joyfully that he does come, indeed that he is here, but now we see how he comes. Each phrase adds a significant dimension to the total picture.

First, two strong uses of the Hebrew word for "Behold" begin the two sets of parallel lines to urge us to sit up and take notice of the way God comes. I am disappointed that the New

Revised Standard Version leaves one of these words out and uses the weaker "see" for the other. The poetic device is the prophet's way of grabbing us by the collar to arouse us from our lethargy and stupidity, our "low information-action ratio" (as Neil Postman calls it in *Amusing Ourselves to Death*). Let us behold how the sovereign *YHWH* comes and entrust our lives to him in response.

Now, it is the "Lord GOD" who comes with might. The Hebrew words are *Adonai YHWH*, sovereign ruler and covenant God. He comes with all the fullness of his paramount lordship, but also as the faithful, promising "I AM." His might is directed toward the fulfilling of his covenant vows, the perfecting of his relationship with his people. Consequently, this phrase was fulfilled as God delivered his people out of the Babylonian captivity. He faithfully kept his promise to restore the remnant.

The first coming of Jesus only partially fulfilled this verse, for he mostly withheld his might, and the rewards of discipleship were, for his followers, mostly unattained in their earthly lives. However, Jesus has promised to come again, and the book of Revelation emphasizes that at that time all his glorious might will fully be made known. Finally, we can look for ways in which God comes as *Adonai YHWH* to us today, a God of might, whose power is channeled to fulfill his promises to us.

How frightful it would be if God exerted his might without the covenant relationship! How terrible God would appear to us if we did not know that his power has its dominion for our benefit! His arm upraised to rule for him would terrify us if we did not know the graciousness of his lordly rule.

Previous verses in Isaiah 40 spoke about the emptiness of human life and its ephemerality, so verse 10 offers a strong contrast in introducing the fullness of God's power. The exaltation and infinity of the LORD's might will be illustrated much more thoroughly later in this fortieth chapter of Isaiah, but these first two phrases in verse 10 offer a brief introduction to the attribute. This phrase reminded the Israelites of their exodus from Egypt, for the foundational events of that deliverance were frequently narrated with the poetic, liturgical, memorized refrain that *YHWH* had done it by "a mighty hand and an outstretched arm" (see, for example, Deuteronomy 4:34; 5:15; 7:19; 9:29; 11:2; 26:8; 1 Kings 8:42; 2 Kings 17:36; 2 Chronicles 6:32).

The second set of parallel phrases in Isaiah 40:10 presents the picture of the Lord GOD bringing gifts with him, though the nature of the reward that is with him is not specified. The Hebrew word means "wages," coming from the root meaning "to hire." The term implies the fulfillment of God's promises to those who serve him. He has promised to his people rewards of present freedom, constant security, ultimate victory, and eternal rest. How different this is from the world's rewards, which depend upon human circumstances right now and eventually pass away.

When our covenant God comes in his power, he brings us the best. As James reminds us, "Every good thing bestowed and every perfect gift is from above, coming down from the Father of lights, with whom there is no variation or shadow of turning" (James 1:17, NAS).

Now, as I prepare the revised edition of this book, I am amazed that even twenty years ago I concentrated so much on God's faithful promising — since only recently have I been thinking about how, in our present postmodern time, this is a fruitful image for showing God to a hopeless world. The great overarching narrative of the Hebrew and Christian Scriptures reveals the Lord GOD as one who always keeps his promises. That invites us to understand our own life story as it is placed into the larger story and to claim God's promises and fulfillments for our own lives. The promise in Isaiah 40 of his coming with might is only partially fulfilled now for us, too, but the resurrection of Jesus and his sending of the Holy Spirit convince us that God's promises can all be trusted for time and for eternity.

The word translated "recompense" in the final phrase of verse 10 carries figurative connotations of a victory procession after warfare, in which *YHWH* parades before him the spoils he has won. Combining the two sets of figures used in this verse, we can imagine the picture in Colossians 2:14-15 of Jesus defeating "the principalities and powers" (in the Revised Standard Version's translation). Not only did he expose their workings at the cross, but he also disarmed them and triumphed over them — destroying their power over us. Consequently, we specifically recognize that the Lord GOD, having defeated the powers, rescued from their grasp all who were enslaved. Thus, his victory procession includes us. When the Lord GOD comes carrying his reward with him, he brings the redeemed ones, the ones rescued out of captivity to sin, the ones delivered from forces that want to control us. And he drives before him, to make a public spectacle of them, all the powers of evil.

One of the best implications of this verse is the strong hope it gives us in our warfare against the principalities and powers of politics, economics, and technological dehumanization. We can trust that our covenant God stands with us, and we know that his might at the cross and the empty tomb defeated all our enemies ultimately. We can enter boldly into any encounters with the powers we might face.[1] We don't have to trust our own power to handle difficulties, for it is the arm of the LORD that rules for him. He has raised that mighty arm on our behalf.

Another image this verse creates is the picture of the Lord

---

1. For a more detailed and thorough look at these "principalities and powers," see Marva J. Dawn, "The Concept of 'the Principalities and Powers' in the Works of Jacques Ellul" (Ph.D. dissertation, University of Notre Dame, 1992).

GOD laden with gifts. He does not come empty-handed. Many people are reluctant to become Christians because they think they will have to give everything up. It's the old false notion that Christians never have any fun. (Why do we Christians give such an impression? Why do we forget resurrection Joy, the Holy-Spirit-empowered Freedom, and the never-disappointing Hope of the gospel?) Imagine the kinds of surprises the LORD carries with him as his rewards!

I am sure each of us has experienced at times the pleasant bewilderment when suddenly the arm of the LORD has been raised for us (like the church leader's defense of me recorded in Chapter 4), or when we have received God's unexpected and totally gracious rewards. Last month at a global mission event I was dumbfounded when two guests from Lebanon gave me the most beautiful stole I'd ever seen — embroidered in gold thread with "I am the Way, the Truth, the Life" in Arabic on one side and with four styles of church steeples on the other!

When I first wrote this book I experienced a similarly stunning surprise. I had gone to my office at the church building for a normal work day, but I suddenly discovered that, since my Hebrew professor would be unavailable to meet with me the following week, it was necessary to travel to Portland immediately to study with him for the background of this manuscript. I was anxious about all the driving (five hours altogether) because of a shortage of sleep the night before and because my eyes were beginning already then to degenerate.

Just as I was getting ready to leave, a close friend stopped by for a quick visit. Because he had not been by for a long time, it was a special treat to see him. Even better, however, was his offer to drive me to Portland. What a coincidence that this day of all days he should come, and what a remarkable gift his contribution of transportation was! Not only did I not have to fight fatigue and vision problems in driving alone, but our conversation was spiritually encouraging for both of us as well. My work with the professor was exciting and rewarding; the scenery of the summer day was especially beautiful. My appreciation for everything all day was heightened by the specific awareness of God's gifts that the particularly surprising endowment of a precious friendship had conveyed.

Two unique illustrations, but not isolated examples, for when we have — and notice — such experiences we understand more deeply the point of this verse. Already we see God using his power on our behalf and bringing his gifts as he comes to us. Some day we will be able to see all his power in all its infinite sovereignty, and the gifts he brings to us then will be eternal.

QUESTIONS FOR FURTHER MEDITATION:

1. What are some of the names for God that especially signify his covenant relationship with his people?

2. How was the arm of the Lord *raised on behalf of his people in the First and Second Testaments? How does remembering these narratives help us?*

3. In what particular ways have I experienced the Lord's *might?*

4. How do we know that the Lord's *might is gracious?*

5. What rewards have I already received in my life?

6. How do we prevent God's rewards (rather than his prior grace) from being the motivation for our service?

7. Why is the overarching narrative of a promising God useful as a response to our culture's postmodern despair because of the failure of modern hopes to solve all our problems?

11 *The Cry of YHWH's Gentleness*

Like a shepherd He will tend His flock,
In His arm He will gather the lambs,
and carry [them] in His bosom,
He will gently lead the nursing [ewes].

Isaiah 40:11 (NAS)

Where is God when you need him? One night almost twenty years ago I discovered the importance of this verse because I needed the gentleness of the LORD's shepherding. I yearned to be able to trust his promise to care for us tenderly.

All evening my heart had been wrapped in a fog of despair. I felt that I had never been treated so cruelly as I had been that night. I begged a person very close to me to accept my love, but my pleas to restore our relationship were rejected with a stony aloofness. My needs for a reconciling touch were shrugged away. Sobbing to the walls, I stumbled to another room and cried out through the window to the sky.

When the tears subsided, I opened my Bible to Isaiah 40 to read the words of comfort in verse 11. "Like one shepherding," the original Hebrew literally begins. Does the mighty God really come to us like that? In our experiences of rejection and failure and other painful sorrows, can we trust this Word and its declarations about YHWH coming like a shepherd? Can there really be such a comfort for me? For you? Yes, I believe it, for it is the Lord GOD who comes.

What a gently loving contrast this verse forms with the preceding one. The same Hebrew word for arm occurs in both, but the arm that ruled and declared God's might in verse 10 now fondly gathers the lambs whom he shepherds. This is a picture to be cherished, for our psyches need both sides of God. We need to know that God exerts his power and strength on our behalf — but we also need to know that in his dealings with us he comes faithfully like a shepherd. Through his Word the Shepherd came dependably and gently to comfort me that night long ago. No doubt you have had moments of excruciating pain or profound sadness, too, when only the mysterious coming of the grace of God enabled you to find genuine relief.

"Like one pasturing, his flock he tends." The nurturing that YHWH provides is doubly emphasized in the Hebrew because the word for "shepherd" comes from the verb root meaning "to feed," and forms of that root both begin and end this phrase. The LORD does not leave us without the means by which we can be nourished. No, instead he carefully provides for our feeding in all situations. A strong hope lies in this promise that wherever we go or whatever we do, as we make use of the means of grace that God provides in his Word and his people, YHWH will sustain us and address our deepest needs. Even on that wrenching night, when there was no one there to comfort me, my longing for God's gentle caring was met by the expressions of comfort in his Word. I write about that situation to invite you to think about what was perhaps the worst, most despairing night of your life. Did you turn to the Bible for comfort? Can we believe that God really does nurture us through the Scriptures?

65

Now, during the time I've been rewriting this book, I've been overwhelmed by the reading I'm doing concerning the onrush of advancements in media technology. I grieve for young people in their twenties and thirties — and even more for the elementary students my husband teaches — who had or have no family interaction, no relational activities in their homes, because everyone is too busy watching television or playing with the computer. The statistics on time for family intimacy are appalling, with spouses spending less than five minutes per day with each other and less than half a minute with their children in conversation. Such behavior, common in U.S. culture, leaves huge holes of yearning in people's lives. And how will the Church fill those gaps with the love of God and the love of the Christian community? I sometimes feel immobilized because churches seem to be failing so badly to offer the Truth of God that our culture so desperately needs. Instead I see clergy grasping for gimmicks to attract the world, studying marketing techniques to make their congregations appealing, reducing worship to entertainment instead of genuine praise of God and formation of the character of believers and the community.

As I thought about those issues upon arising this morning, I turned to the Moravian Texts for morning devotions, and the first text for the day was Psalm 42:11:

> Why are you cast down, O my soul,
>   and why are you disquieted within me?
> Hope in God; for I shall again praise him,
>   my help and my God.

After meditating on how effectively this assigned reading suited my need for this time of profound concern (does God change the bookmarks, I often wonder?), I thanked God for the precious solace of that psalm and then turned to the hymn for the day. It was this marvelous text:

O God, our help in ages past,
our hope for years to come,
our shelter from the stormy blast,
and our eternal home!

The rest of the verses from that hymn continued the mystery of
the morning — the ineffable wonder that God clearly speaks to
us in his Word and in the faith of the community passed on
through hymns and the silences of devotional times. Do we open
our lives often enough and thoroughly enough to the Shepherd's
caring provision?

One of my students at the University of Idaho had worried
about what would happen when he left the school and was no
longer exposed to the Bible studies and fellowship available on
campus. Months after he left, however, he came back to visit and
announced that in every place to which he had gone, God had
provided for his spiritual needs.

Another student experienced the same thing even more
dramatically. As he left for graduate work elsewhere he recognized
the importance of biblical nurturing. Deliberately becoming involved in a discipling relationship with his roommate, who was
newly a Christian, he found his own faith immeasurably strengthened. Soon he became a leader among the Christians on that
campus, and now, as I observe him many years later in his
marriage and in a highly demanding professional career, I am
amazed at the outstanding Christian leader he has become.

With what variety and thoroughness the LORD provides
so that his people are fed! He nurtures us through the disciplines
of our own devotional times and private meditations. He propels
us by means of teachers and preachers and practitioners of his
Word. He sustains us through the vitality of Christian communities and assemblies of believers. He nourishes us through music.
He uplifts us with breathtaking sunsets and the myriad hues of

flowers. Truly, the LORD, our shepherd, endows us so that we shall not want.

The second phrase in verse 11 tells us that God not only feeds us but also gathers us up in his arms. "I am Jesus' little lamb" we sang when I was a child, and still the image comforts me, though I'm not too thrilled when I consider the stupidity of lambs and the suggestion that I fit that characterization. Yet when we face the realities of our lives, we have to admit that we often act just like sheep. But there is more to the picture than just the foolishness of the lamb.

The appeal of this picture is the promise that we can really be protected. When we are worried about the criticism we are getting in our work or about whether things will turn out all right in the building project we are working on, we want to feel sure somehow that we are safeguarded and secure. Don't you sometimes need to be sheltered? Whether you are male or female, young or old, I am sure that at certain times you long to feel safe and held.

My husband Myron teaches me that about God. When I feel so defenseless against undue reproach and vulnerable to professional attacks, he holds me — and he asks for the same from me. Together we can remember that when we feel so empty and small, we need more than anything to be wrapped up in God's arms and securely enfolded in his love. That is the delight to me of the name Habakkuk, which means "God's love-embrace."

A loving spouse is nonetheless inadequate to illustrate Isaiah 40's picture of God, for we are not embraced only individually, in isolation. Verse 11 declares that God gathers the lambs, and the noun is used plurally only here in the First Testament. (The singular form in its Aramaic version is the basis for the word *Talitha,* which Jesus said to Jairus's daughter in Mark 5:41, though our translations usually render the term of endearment, *Talitha cum,* "little girl, arise" instead of "little lamb, arise.")

The modern term for a collective community, the Jewish

kibbutz, comes from the verb used here for gathering. This Word of God is made real — incarnated today — in the fellowship of Christian believers. During all my single years and still today I experience God's love-embrace especially through the care, affection, and security provided by my friends in Christ. One of the most significant dimensions of our worshiping communities must be this kind of spiritual embrace to enfold everyone, especially those who are alone, in the tangible love of God.

When those who participate in the "gathering" express their relationship to us with a gentle touch and with practical, tangible care, God's embrace is made even more real. But too often churches fail to provide the comforting and genuine nurturing this embrace entails. Recently a pastoral couple with a severely handicapped daughter bemoaned to me that their Christian "community" had utterly failed to give them the support they needed. The security of being God's beloved people together *could* be thoroughly offered to all and by all who participate in each assembly of believers. How could our churches more thoroughly become and live as true communities?[1]

The last two phrases of verse 11 amplify the picture. The LORD lifts up the lambs to carry them in his bosom or in the fold of his garment. Here the Hebrew verb we translate "to carry" is the same one that described the lifting up of the valleys in verse 4. The Shepherd lifts us out of our valleys of despair and difficulty to carry us close to his heart. Furthermore, the Shepherd gently leads those that are with young. The verb translated "leads" implies in the Hebrew a bringing to a place of rest or a watering place. That implication reinforces again the feeding and nurturing stressed at the beginning of the verse.

These last two phrases imply a significant progression — from being a young one, carried, to being a ewe-with-young,

1. For suggestions and practical questions for discussion, see Marva J. Dawn, *The Hilarity of Community: Romans 12 and How to Be the Church* (Grand Rapids: Wm. B. Eerdmans, 1992).

nurtured and guided. When we are young and not able to walk, *YHWH* lifts us up and furnishes the transportation. When we are older and don't know which direction to go, he shows us the way. We don't know how to walk in the freedom of the Christian life unless we have first been carried by grace. We must begin by resting in the LORD and allowing him to do everything on our behalf (that is, forgiving us, giving us new life, transforming us). With that essential foundation of grace, we then learn to live out the freedom of our faith.

We must first be carried by the Shepherd before we are able to bear young ourselves. As the Shepherd gathers us into the community of saints in the beginning of our life of faith, we must rely totally on the nurturing of Christ through his Body of believers. Christ and the community carry us and provide for all our needs. Then, as our faith grows, we become equipped to nurture others. We might become the spiritual parents for the birth of new Christians, though still we ourselves will rely totally on God's leading.

It seems to me that much of the weakness of churches in our present culture in the United States exists because this seemingly simplistic progression is ignored. New believers are nurtured inadequately. More experienced believers are not actively involved in birthing young by passing on the faith. And grace is not the foundation for it all. We can't be mother ewes and nourish our young-in-faith unless we are directly following the Shepherd.

The reason that the Christian community does not grow is not because our worship services aren't entertaining enough (as many clergy mistakenly think these days),[2] but because the process has been truncated. Lambs are growing up without becoming parents.

The life proclaimed in verse 11 begins with the need for

2. See Marva J. Dawn, *Reaching Out without Dumbing Down: A Theology of Worship for the Turn-of-the-Century Culture* (Grand Rapids: Wm. B. Eerdmans, 1995).

total submission to the feeding of God. Then it invites us to devoted, intimate following of YHWH's way so that we can be mothers who give birth to new faith. Notice that the Shepherd does not lead us with the might of the previous verse. Instead, he leads us gently, so that we want to follow. His compassionate guidance stirs in us the desire to pass on his affectionate nurturing to those who are spiritually in our care.

The New Jerusalem Bible translates the verse's last phrase "leading to their rest the mother ewes." This is God's supreme promise for our Christian lives: The Shepherd is always leading us to our ultimate rest. Grace always undergirds our whole lives all along the journey, and the one who declares himself the Good Shepherd (John 10:11, 14) also claims to be the Way (John 14:6) for eternal reconciliation and reunion with God.

QUESTIONS FOR FURTHER MEDITATION:

1. How can this verse be helpful to me in times of depression, doubt, or fear?

2. Through what means can I receive the spiritual feeding the Shepherd wants to provide me? How can I experience more thoroughly the security of God's love-embrace?

3. Why do I often run away from the means by which he nurtures or embraces me?

4. In what ways do I try to make it on my own as a lamb or as a mother ewe?

5. Whom has the Shepherd committed to my spiritual care?

6. How might I make better use of God's means of grace to follow him more faithfully and to nurture more effectively the young in my care?

7. Do the members of my Christian community all see themselves as potential mothers-in-the-faith? Are we multiplying ourselves by passing on the faith to our children, our neighbors, our colleagues?

12 *Our Cry of Wonder*

Who has measured the waters in the hollow of his hand
and marked off the heavens with a span,
enclosed the dust of the earth in a measure,
and weighed the mountains in scales
and the hills in a balance?

Isaiah 40:12

First, imagine all the raindrops in the world. Then add all the snowflakes and hailstones, the fog and the mists. Next, bring in all the creeks and ponds and puddles. Finally, add all the glaciers and snow packs, the streams and rivers, the wells and underground springs, and even all the lakes and the mammoth oceans. All the waters of the earth, added together — and God holds them in a single handful! Inconceivable!

Whereas in verse 11 we saw the gentleness of God, now in verse 12 we catch a glimpse of God's astonishing transcendence. I love the way the images of the Hebrew faith are so tangible. Though we must use great care when we anthropomorphically assign human qualities and characteristics to God so that we might better understand him, we have to use such images in order to begin to comprehend what cannot ever be fully known. Images such as these of weighing and measuring enable us at least to notice the infinity of God's greatness — and yet, after all the profound pictures and the application of these minute measurements to magnificent things, we begin to realize the incomprehensibility of our subject. Even to suggest that we can start to grasp the character and extent of God's sovereignty is absurd.

The entire verse is set up as a rhetorical question based on the initial interrogative pronoun, *who?* Of course, there is only one answer. The Lord GOD is the only one capable of such feats. Each phrase is valuable, however, for stirring up a deeper wonder, for filling us with astonishment at the inconceivable dominion of God.

"Who has measured the waters in the hollow of his hand?" Even if we limited our picture to just one of the bodies of water mentioned at the beginning of this chapter, the image is mind-boggling. Try to imagine a person holding the Pacific Ocean in the palm of her hand. Having grown up in landlocked Ohio and living now not far from the Pacific, I am like a child when I stand on its vast shores. Who can but be overwhelmed by its thundering waves, its myriad forms of life, its infinite variety of hues — the multifaceted splendor of the sea? Just to begin to think about the size is an arresting experience. But then to go one step further and imagine the Lord GOD holding that in the palm of a single hand is superlatively staggering.

The Hebrew form that we translate "hollow of his hand" occurs only three times in the First Testament. In the other two places it is plural, referring to handfuls, such as in the phrase, "handfuls of barley." Only in Isaiah 40:12 is the word singular to impress us with how astounding this is. God needs only one hand to hold all that water. And even as we are dumbfounded by that picture, we realize how inadequate it is, for God created all that

73

water with just his Word. Because the poet suggests the picture, however, to study it even in its inadequacy gives us a little better idea of the tremendous might and power the Lord GOD possesses.

The second picture in this verse makes us laugh. The measure of a span is the distance between the end of one's little finger and of one's thumb when the hand is fully spread. That equals the distance of one-half a cubit. Imagine God — it is even funnier if we picture that ridiculous caricature of Father Time, with a long, white beard and a cane — establishing whole galaxies by the spanful! Whole light years of space are encompassed by his fingers. I wonder how many solar systems can be hidden under his little finger nail!

The verb form of this second phrase actually means "to mete out" or "to make right according to the standard." Thus, together with the initial interrogative pronoun of the verse assumed here, this phrase asks, "Who regulated the heavens by the span?" The humorous picture forces us to laugh at our silly stupidity: If God is capable of doing such a thing, aren't we foolish not to trust him? Aren't we obtuse not to realize that this power will be exercised on our behalf by our covenant God? (See Chapter 10.) Whereas human beings measure the distance between stars in light years (a measurement too immense to imagine), God determines those same spaces with the distance between his thumb and his pinky (an image too incredible in its inadequacy).

The third phrase of verse 12 says literally, "and all in the third part the dust of the earth." There is no verb in this phrase, and the unit of measurement is thought by most scholars to mean the third part of an ephah, or about a quarter of a gallon. All the sands of the ocean beaches, all the dust in your house and mine, all the dirt that all kids everywhere bring home from their play — all the soil of the earth God can hold, or measure, in his strawberry bucket.

And then, as if that weren't demonstration enough, he

weighs all the mountains in a single scale and all the hills in a double balance. Now both the terms of elevation in verse 4 are used again here in the plural to assert that God assesses them critically.

This last picture is the funniest of all to me. Imagine, if you will, a single scale sitting on a table. And there is God, tossing on Mount McKinley, Mount Everest, all the Himalayas, K2, the Alps, the Rockies and the Tetons, the Cascades and the Appalachians, Mount Kilamanjaro and what's left of Mount Saint Helen's — and then assessing their worth! Having once lived close to Mount Rainier, I found it fascinating that we could drive for hours and not seem to get any closer to that magisterial peak. Once, while coming back from the east side of the Washington Cascades, we suddenly rounded a curve, and there, right in front of us in all its glory, towered Mount Rainier, four or five times taller than I would have expected it to be. And yet, the prophet insists, the Lord GOD easily picks up that mountain and, with a flick of his wrist, tosses it on the scale!

I'm sure that at this point you are realizing with me the utter ludicrousness of our human perceptions. We can't even begin to imagine what God is like; all our pictures are shockingly dazzling, and yet they don't even scratch the surface of the unutterable wonder of his inexpressible infinity. Why are we such blind fools in our presumptions that we do not trust this God who exercises his might on our behalf? "Who can do these things?" Isaiah 40 asks, and the galaxies sing out the answer. Indeed, "the heavens are telling the glory of God; and the firmament proclaims his handiwork" (Psalm 19:1). How, then, shall we respond?

QUESTIONS FOR FURTHER MEDITATION:

1. *What images might I use to describe the infinity of God?*
2. *What does this verse teach me about the character of God?*

3. What does this verse teach me about myself?

4. Why are these pictures of God's inconceivable majesty not terrifying?

5. When measurements of such trivial size refer to such vast entities, how do I feel? What emotions do I experience thinking about this verse?

6. How can verses such as this be used to deepen the praises of my worship?

7. What are the implications of this verse for the world?

13 Our Cry for the Counselor

*Who has directed the spirit of the LORD,
or as his counselor has instructed him?*

Isaiah 40:13

I was terribly disappointed and awfully confused. Health problems at the time I graduated from college had prevented my
accepting a teaching position in Hong Kong. I thought, perhaps,
that I should go on to graduate school, but I had not received
any of the scholarships or fellowships for which I'd been a nom-
inee. Nothing seemed to fit together. I'd received one offer to
teach English while doing graduate work at the University of
Idaho, but it didn't make much sense to go there so far from my
home in Ohio and without knowing anyone.

"Now, God," I seemed to be saying in my prayers, "are
you sure you know all the facts?" I figured that if he had all the
facts straight, he would certainly do things my way. What folly
and presumption! Who would dare to think that God needs our
advisement?

Rhetorically, the prophet poses the same question in Isaiah

77

40:13. He asks who has directed the Spirit of *YHWH* or as his counselor has instructed him. Obviously the answer is that no one can, that no one does, and yet how often we do try.

The first question in the Hebrew is made doubly ironic by the occurrence of a repeated verb; the same verb that was chosen to describe God's regulating of the heavens in verse 12 asks now who it is that establishes God. Can anyone have the ability to direct him, he who directed the ordering of the heavens with his thumb and little finger? When will we learn to take seriously the magnificence of God?

The word for *Spirit* bears many noteworthy connotations in the First Testament. It signifies the powerful agent through whom God has done his creative work. The LORD's Spirit brings life and makes us all alive; he brought order out of chaos. Who could dare to try to order him?

The form of the verb in the poetic parallel of the second line doubly reinforces the folly of anyone pictured by these two questions. Who has thought that she could cause God to be instructed by her counsel? Who can stand by as if wise enough to enlighten the one who is himself called by the name of "Wonderful Counselor" (Isaiah 9:6)?

Down through the ages, these words in Isaiah have mocked the folly of those who presume to instruct the Spirit of the LORD. Many people during the Babylonian captivity must have thought that they knew the best way to restore God's people from their exile. It took men like Ezra and Nehemiah, faithful leaders who listened to instruction from *YHWH*, to stir up the people to reconstruct the city of Jerusalem and its temple, to rebuild the walls and restore the nation according to God's plan.

Peter tried to instruct Jesus on how to fulfill his office by rebuking him when he prophesied his suffering and death (Matthew 16:21-23). How little Peter understood that through shame and sorrow instead of power and splendor God would fulfill his purposes, not just for rescuing the people of Israel from Roman rule, but for the whole world.

Similarly, how little we understand the purposes of God for our lives and, through us, for others. Our perspectives are severely limited. How often don't we try to instruct the LORD instead of waiting for his direction, instead of submitting to his perfect will. We pray as if we had to straighten God around. In our presumptions we think we can know what is best for us, choose how our lives should develop, and control our own futures.

What idolatry this verse points out in our lives! We probably think this way far more often than we admit. How often do we have the audacity to assume that we really can grasp all the elements that comprise our existence, that we actually can see far more than the God who reigns in the heavens and marks them off with the span of his hand?

We might ask, then, about the value of prayer. Why should we spend time putting into words our feelings and concerns or our needs and cares? The LORD knows them all anyway. He doesn't need our instruction. He knows perfectly well who we are, how we feel, and what we desire. Does this verse indirectly negate the value of prayer?

Certainly not — especially since prayer is decidedly more a matter of relationship than of words. One of the gifts of prayer for me arises from this very fact that the LORD does not need anyone to counsel him. In our words of praise, we remember his power and sovereignty. We are reminded of his infinite wisdom and care, and consequently we are assured that he is watching over everything that concerns us (1 Peter 5:7) and that he will work all things together for our good (Romans 8:28).

Furthermore, as we unfold to him our perceptions of ourselves and others, we find them deepened and clarified. He has promised to give wisdom to those who ask (James 1:5-8).

Orthodox Bishop Kallistos Ware suggests that prayer is "listening in to the conversation of the Trinity" to gather insights and to know we are beloved.

In our petitions and intercessions, our own desperation because of our weakness and sin is made more clear. We can come to recognize as we pray for God's action on behalf of others that he wants to use us for the fulfilling of his purposes. What better picture of grace is there than this: No one directs the Spirit of the LORD and no one can be his instructor, yet he deigns to use us and to make us valuable members of his body to effect his will on the earth. In his perfection he hears our cry and comes to comfort us, to give us guidance, and to instruct us in ways we can serve his purposes.

In the New Testament unveiling of the Trinity, the Spirit of the LORD is recognized as Paraclete (or the "called-alongside-one," John 14:16). Jesus promised his disciples that the Spirit would be sent in order for them to continue his work — with even greater works. Now that the Spirit has been poured out upon, and indwells, each one of us personally, we can truly find counsel, especially in mutual listening as the Spirit speaks through members of the corporate Christian community.

Although in this short meditation we can't outline a thorough description of the Spirit-filled and Spirit-led life, we can allow this verse to stir up in us a greater desire for such an existence. We can be encouraged to seek the Holy Spirit's counsel through the discernment of the Christian community. The irony of the prophet's questions pinpoints our major problem — that we are not as directed by the Spirit as we could be because too often we are trying too hard to direct him. When we insist upon our own perceptions and mastery, we cannot be open enough to see and hear and feel the insights, commands, and nudges the Spirit is trying to give us. The help of other Christians is vital for waking us up to God's revelations.

The example noted at the beginning of this chapter made this truth clear in a lovely and surprising way. After I was denied health clearance to teach in Hong Kong, I had to choose between teaching in a Lutheran high school and going on to graduate school. I had prayed that if the latter was what I should do the finances would be provided. I agonized over the decision until the very day before leaving for Easter vacation, the time when I had to tell the college placement officer whether I would take a call to teach. I hadn't won a fellowship, and I was stupidly blind to God's way of providing the finances. Not until a caring professor woke me up to see God's design in the University of Idaho's offer of an instructional assistantship was my decision clear. I wound up teaching "Literature of the Bible" in the English Department and immediately became involved in leading a Bible study for high school students. Almost a year later, I was asked by one of the youth when I had made my decision to come to Idaho. I reported the exact day, and she shook her head in wonder. That was the very time that she and her friends had prayed that God would send them a Bible study leader. I don't believe such things are mere coincidences — but I had almost missed the Spirit's direction because I had previously decided how the finances for my graduate study ought to be obtained.

"Who has directed the Spirit of the LORD?" Isaiah 40 asks. No one has. And no one can. Maybe you and I should give up trying.

QUESTIONS FOR FURTHER MEDITATION:

1. What have been some times when I have tried to direct the LORD *according to my own perceptions of things?*

2. What were some situations in which I discovered clear direction from God concerning my life?

3. What were some situations in which the Christian community helped me to recognize clearer instructions from the Spirit?

4. How can I learn to listen more carefully to the Spirit?

5. How can my life become more specifically directed by God's purposes?

6. How specifically does God direct me? Does he have a plan for my moment-by-moment existence, or does he give a more general direction in which I should go, leaving me to make my own decisions on the way? What scriptural evidence is there for my opinion?

7. What is the relationship of my free will to God's direction by means of the Spirit's guidance?

14 *The Cry of God's Understanding*

With whom did He consult and [who] gave Him understanding?
and [who] taught Him in the path of justice
and taught Him knowledge,
and informed Him of the way of understanding?

Isaiah 40:14 (NAS)

My pleading with her was in vain. She lived across the hall from me in a graduate student apartment dorm. I begged her with all the love I had to reconsider her decision to move in with her boyfriend. She went anyway, but in a few weeks she was back. He had dumped her, and she had discovered with grievous sorrow that "If it feels good, do it" was not a workable philosophy of life.

"Life, liberty, and the pursuit of happiness!" "Reason, nature, and progress!" And now the postmodern "Random, play, and deconstruction" (which means, more or less, chaos). Throughout the history of civilization such slogans have promoted particular lifestyles or philosophies or governments as the means to happiness and fulfillment. Each historical period of enlightenment has been characterized by a grand optimism, a conviction that human beings have become more reasonable and wise and therefore will be able to solve all our problems. But the euphoria of the 1960s that the student rebels could fix our society has given way to the nihilistic gloom of many "boomers" in the 1990s and a rising "blank generation" that can't find meaning in anything beyond the next mode of entertainment. One can't help but observe that every historical era of rapturous optimism has been followed by a time when people have recognized that their science or reason, their amassed fortunes or technology, cannot transport them to the heights they had envisioned. The euphoria crashes, and the next period is marked by a severe decline in morality and justice — humanity destroying itself. Our postmodern era is just such a regression into despairing and desperate violence and a hopelessness manifested by the perpetual adolescence of thrill-seekers. After all the fanfare, the brazen presumptuousness of the glory of human progress, comes the crushing realization that people are, despite their pretensions, not so smart after all.

On the other hand, says the prophet, look at God. Whom did he consult for his understanding? The rhetorical question forces us to admit that the epitome of enlightenment — in fact, the only true enlightenment — comes from *YHWH*. Each time human beings have turned back to God in the spirit of repentance, revival, and reform, there has followed a time of great moral endeavor, a building of genuine justice in the society.

Consider, for example, the tremendous humanitarian deeds that followed the Wesleyan revival, such as the abolition of slavery, the securing of better working conditions, and the elimination of child labor. Following the Word of the One who needs no one else to give him understanding will result in clearer insight and deeper awareness of both the problems of society and the means for solving those problems. Human enlightenment, on the other hand, ultimately causes human beings only to turn to ourselves in exaltation of our own reason. Now the postmodern rejection of truth and meaning and reason underscores the failure of human myths about our brilliance and progress. In the midst of this milieu, we who believe in the covenant God of the Bible have a superb opportunity to offer to the world around us the great gift of a God whose understanding is perfect.

The second question in Isaiah 40:14 asks us, "Who has taught *YHWH* in the path of justice?" Here again we are roused to survey our world, and we are forced to admit that genuine and thorough justice is nowhere to be found. As long as we are under the control of a human nature that wants to seek the best for the self, we will ultimately deal unjustly with others. Recognizing that true justice is possible only in the freedom from self found in total devotion and obedience to Another, we hunger and thirst after his righteousness.

"Who has taught *YHWH* knowledge?" The Hebrew phrase, best rendered by the Jerusalem Bible's "Who has discovered for him the most skillful way?" actually emphasizes workmanship or creative proficiency. Does God need instruction to invent new forms, to compose new sounds, to fabricate new materials, to produce what is right and best?

This morning I have been listening to the exquisite *Requiem* of Maurice Duruflé, set for choir, organ, and small orchestra. Such amazing sounds he composed, under the influence of Gregorian chant, the elegant French classical school, impressionism, and polyphonic Renaissance choral music. Even the buildings of the Church — the physical, spiritual, and emotional ambience of cathedrals and their liturgies — are seen by scholars as sources for his lush and lofty creations. However, as I listen, I can't help but realize that his immense craftsmanship, as well as the trained skills of the performing musicians, all originate in the mind of God. Harmonies so heavenly, melodies so metaphysical, con-

85

trapuntal so celestial lifts us beyond the proficiency of human vessels to the Originator of all capabilities and craft.

"Who has taught him the way of understanding?" is the final question of verse 14. The last noun in the Hebrew text is derived from the same root as the initial verb of the verse, so it ties all four phrases together with the initial "Who." The term signifies reason, but it is used here in a plural form to indicate the faculties for all understanding and insight, logic and thought. It suggests true enlightenment and questions whether anyone can show God the way to it. As with all the verse's queries, the answer is obvious: Only God possesses perfect understanding.

How often we hear the cry for understanding! Teenagers rebelling against their parents scream, "You don't understand me!" Liberated wives leaving their husbands angrily accuse them of the same. Rioters in prisons and violent troublemakers in high schools condemn the lack of empathy on the part of institutional authorities. Sometimes the lament is soft and pleading and lonely. Youngsters in my husband's elementary school classes exhibit instinctive symptoms of the alienation and estrangement of our times.

Into this picture comes the LORD. Not needing anyone to teach him how to understand, he has known each of us from before our conception. Can we comprehend that he embraces our personality traits and foibles, discerns our deepest needs, unravels our confusions? His immense love for us charts the twists and turns of our minds, delights in the desires of our hearts, and distinguishes the conflicting feelings of our souls. Truly he understands us infinitely better than we can ourselves.

Why do we doubt, then? When we turn to him, why do we think we won't be completely understood? Don't we yet comprehend that God knows all the intricacies of our situations and cares immensely for what matters to us most?

We've all known people who are so supremely gifted in

their chosen fields that it seems they never need to be taught. What they do best they do with such skill that it seems automatic. With seemingly no effort they concoct gourmet food, shape perceptive poems, or master complicated computer terminology and technology. This work is easy for them because it is of their very nature to cook or write or travel cyberspace. They freely give expression to their essential being.

Stretch that freedom now to infinity to exult in the character of God. How could we ever be understood more deeply than by the One whose very character is to understand, to be just, to have all skill?

The immensity of God's wisdom and understanding and insight is a tremendous source of comfort for us. Most of us struggle continually with the terrible tension of trying to keep all the dimensions of our lives in balance. We don't know how all at once to be a spouse or a single person, a parent involved with the kids' activities or a social activist, a servant of the Church or of society, and a human being — and yet we believe we are called to fulfill each of these roles and many more. Sometimes we get frustrated because we don't have any models — women with our professional interests, students with our particular struggles, pastors with our specific burdens. Often we feel misunderstood by caring friends who try to give advice, but who don't know all the factors that affect our decisions about how best to be good stewards of our time and abilities.

Meanwhile, the slogans that human beings devise deceive us. The lifestyles promoted by the culture that encroaches upon us betray us. Following the gurus of the times, we travel dead-end streets. And presumptuous rejections of God's answers prove disastrous for us.

Does God really guide us with his Spirit? Can we learn to listen to his wisdom?

Isaiah 40 teaches us who this God is whose guidance can

be trusted. Its rhetorical questions confront us with the folly of our blind assumption that God is not able to handle all our needs or that he does not care about them.

What peace it gives us to realize all the ways in which the LORD communicates to us his wisdom and understanding. His Word offers the clearest picture of genuine justice. The Christian community together hears the Spirit of the true Counselor to give us insight for our decisions. Our personal prayer and devotional lives enable us to perceive directions for better balance and greater wholeness in our lives. The discovery of new skills that God fashioned in us often ushers us into fresh avenues of interest and service.

I long to be more attentive to the Counselor, and I pray that the words of this chapter have stirred in you, too, a desire to trust more fully God's perfect understanding. The One who needs no one to teach him or to give him counsel longs to be gracious to us (Isaiah 30:18). How blessed we are if we reject the world's empty philosophies (Colossians 2:8) and learn from him (Matthew 11:29)!

QUESTIONS FOR FURTHER MEDITATION:

1. *What things about myself confuse me? What inexplicable behaviors have surprised me lately?*

2. *How does it help me to know that God knows and understands everything?*

3. *What other passages from the Scriptures show me that God understands?*

4. *How is the justice of the LORD different from that of the world?*

5. *How does my faith help me to adjust to the rapid proliferation of knowledge in our culture?*

6. How can I strengthen my congregation to be a community in which we truly help each other discern the guidance of the Holy Spirit?

7. What tools or skills could I use in my personal devotional life to help me listen more carefully to God's instruction?

15 *The Cry against Nationalism*

Behold, the nations are like a drop from a bucket,
and are regarded as a speck of dust on the scales;
Behold, He lifts up the islands like fine dust.

Isaiah 40:15 (NAS)

We just can't get the very last drop. Whether we're trying to pour oil from a can, juice from a pitcher, or water from a bucket, that last drop usually refuses to fall. It's too tiny. Not enough remains to gather itself together to pour over the side. It doesn't weigh enough to make it over the lip of the container. Finally we give up. That last drop is inconsequential anyway.

That is the picture Isaiah 40 uses to describe the nations. They are as trifling as a meager drop hanging from the lip of a bucket. With a similar "Behold!" to the pair that introduced the Lord GOD in verse 10, the prophet cries for us to notice them. The Hebrew noun for "nations" is very much like the Greek word *ethnos* (from which we get "ethnic"). It means "the people" and carries connotations of societies apart from the chosen people, Gentiles as contrasted with the Israelites. It can signify political entities, but it does not necessarily stress their governments as does our modern word *nations*.

The uniqueness of the image the prophet selects to describe the nations is underscored by his deliberate choice of rare terms. The word translated "drop" is used only here in the entire First Testament; the noun rendered "bucket" is used elsewhere only once, in the book of Numbers. The phrase is introduced by a word of comparison and reads literally, "like a drop from a bucket." The Jerusalem Bible graphically captures its hanging with its version, "like a drop on the pail's rim."

The poetic parallel of the second line paints the nations even smaller. "As a fine dust on the balance they are reckoned." We just blow that dust away — and if some of it remains on the scales, it won't matter anyway. The dust is of no account whatsoever, too fine and light to distort the weighing.

"Behold," the prophet says again, "the islands are so small that the LORD lifts them up as if they were pulverized." The verb here is closely related in sound to another verb that means to cast or to hurl; perhaps a pun is intended. God can pick up the coastlands as if they were fine powder. He might hurl dust into the sea and create new islands. The point, of course, is that nations and peoples who think they are important are really minuscule in relation to the sovereignty of the Lord GOD. The message is not vindictive or vengeful; it merely illustrates again the colossal preeminence of *YHWH*.

This verse is as profoundly appropriate in our time as it was in the days of the prophets of Israel. The twentieth century has constantly, brutally, in myriad escalating clashes fulfilled Jesus' prophecy that "nation will rise against nation, and kingdom against kingdom" (Matthew 24:7-8 and parallels). The media bombard us with reports of the arming and warring of nations, the termination of nations, the revolt of nations against their rulers, the civil wars that rip nations apart, the accusations of one

91

nation against another, and — rarely — the seeking of peace between nations. The nation-state is one of the major idolatries of
our times — as demonstrated so powerfully in the bitter ethnic
cleansing of the former Yugoslavia and in the twin lands of
Rwanda and Burundi.

The prophet's "Behold" in verse 15 stirs us to sit up and pay
attention to this pertinent word of warning and compelling word
of comfort that the nations are merely a drop on the bucket rim.
The warning is especially germane against the pride of the United
States in its present world position. Having such vast resources at
our disposal, including great minds and willing workers to use and
develop those resources, U.S. society tends more and more to claim
it all for ourselves as if we had no responsibility to a needy world.
(Of the top twenty industrialized nations of the world, the U.S.
gives the lowest percentage in aid to poorer countries.) Then we
protect what is "ours" with our enormous weapons systems and
military arsenals. Consequently, we are caught in a physical captivity of things, the emotional enslavement of our fear of losing them,
and the spiritual slavery of that idolatry.

The Israelites at the time of Isaiah were very proud; they
were confident of their own capabilities as a nation and of their
status as the chosen people. Soon, however, their confidence was
threatened by the siege of Sennacherib, and later that confidence
was shattered as they were taken away into exile. We in the United
States must also beware lest the power we depend upon in world-
wide affairs is suddenly revealed as the illusion it truly is. In an
airport as I traveled home from teaching in Norway I heard a
news report about the enormous vulnerability of the United States
since so much depends on computers (and Swedish hackers had
recently invaded the CIA's Web site). Loss of respect for the
United States has spanned the globe for decades, and the moral
feebleness of our government and its policies leads to distrust
and antagonism that resound throughout the world.

Already when I was on our college choir world mission tour, I saw the contempt of much of the world for the United States. In many nations that we visited in the Orient, the Middle East, and Europe, I was astounded at the hatred with which people from the United States were greeted. It was only after learning a few fragments of sentences in the local language and only when I walked away by myself to get acquainted with the cities that I was able to get a better understanding of the peoples we visited. Before that, their general hostility against a tour group of "Americans" was overwhelming. I wanted to communicate, to learn, to become a friend. What gave rise to their angry reactions?

I learned that they had experienced so many repulsive tourists with all their rudeness and gluttony, their haughtiness and condescension, and their endless demands for every respect and service that the local citizens suspected everyone from the United States of having similar attitudes toward them. I don't blame them. I didn't see much concern and love on the part of many tourists either, and at times I was ashamed of the insensitivity and materialism that I caught in myself.

I am grateful that many agencies are developing various kinds of "reverse tourism," such as Ministry of Money's eye-opening visits to lands of poverty, Christian Palestinians' alternative tours of the Holy Land, or Witness for Peace's vigils for assisting the resettlement of refugees. Mennonite colleges customarily require all their students to spend at least one term in a Two-Thirds World country where they join residents in service projects. Our own college mission tour gave all the proceeds from our concerts to local churches for their ministries and brought new world awareness to all of us who participated.

I am not an alarmist or a pessimist or a cynic, but surely the time is overdue for Christians of every nation to assert our primary allegiance to the Kingdom of God and consequently to reevaluate our attitudes toward the policies of our nation-states.

93

This does not mean that we retreat to a privatized ghetto; it means instead that we, as members primarily of God's family, dare not put our trust in the governments of this world to bring about genuine justice or to solve the problems of humanity. Jacques Ellul calls such reliance "the political illusion," since human governments, too, are fallible and flawed. We have learned from previous verses that "all flesh is grass." Nations shall pass away. They are as inconsequential as dust.

On the other hand, this verse also contains a tremendous word of hope, especially in this time of racial, political, and religious tensions among various peoples of the world. When we feel immobilized by ethnic cleansing, government hostility and posturing, the threat of environmental deterioration or of nuclear skirmishes initiated by small upstart nations, it is a great comfort for those of us who seek to counteract some of these situations in the world that the nations are a drop in a bucket. Ultimately God is LORD of all nations; his love is larger than their hate.

We have seen God's love at work in the deposing of the Marcos regime in the Philippines, in the Velvet Revolution of the Czech Republic, in the peaceful election of Nelson Mandela in South Africa. But these examples are too few.

God's people everywhere need to rise above nationalism and ethnic hatred to seek and to build the peace that surmounts these forces. Human peace efforts are not enough — though they are useful. We need the peace of God.

In God we place our trust, not in governments or weapons, nor in peoples or nations. There is hope for the world only because God is sovereign. The nations are fine powders and mere drops on a pail's rim in relation to *YHWH*.

QUESTIONS FOR FURTHER MEDITATION:

1. *At what times has my nation experienced a revival in its awareness of its inconsequentiality in relation to God, and what has happened during those times?*

2. *How can I be influential to change the attitudes of my nation about itself? (This question does not intend to suggest that Christians impose their perspectives on the public, but that, as a minority, we offer the world around us genuine, workable alternatives.)*

3. *What might a foreign policy guided by Christian principles look like?*

4. *What attitudes should control my behavior when I am a guest of other peoples?*

5. *In what conflicts in the history of the world have I seen the* LORD's *hand at work?*

6. *In what ways can I help to build peace in the world?[1]*

7. *How can I help others to find their "national security" in the* LORD *rather than in the leaders or weapons of this world?*

---

1. See the suggestions in chapter 28, "Striving for Peace," in Marva J. Dawn, *The Hilarity of Community: Romans 12 and How to Be the Church* (Grand Rapids: Wm. B. Eerdmans, 1992), pp. 262-70.

16 The Cry of Our Offering's Inadequacy

Lebanon would not provide fuel enough,
nor are its animals enough for a burnt offering.

Isaiah 40:16

A million baby trees in three greenhouses — they look like a carpet of inch-high grass. But imagine what they will be like in eighty years when they forest part of a mountain top.

An acquaintance who worked supervising the greenhouses of the Washington Department of Natural Resources showed me how the seeds were planted in carrot-shaped containers so that their roots could wrap around the soil. Once established, the greenhouse trees can then be used for reforestation after harvesting or after a forest fire. The DNR's work gave me a much better appreciation for the vast number of cedar trees that once clothed Lebanon. I have seen how much time and effort it takes to raise the trees to cover just a small section of land.

Isaiah 40 pokes fun at the inadequacy of all offerings to YHWH by an indirect reference to the trees of Lebanon. The prophet's comments in the original Hebrew are elliptical: "Lebanon not enough for burning; its beasts not enough for a burnt offering." This is such a tangible picture of the insufficiency of any sacrifices. Consider the ancient country of Lebanon, how it was known far and wide for its beautiful cedars, how Solomon imported vast treasures of its precious wood to build the temple and his palaces. All the wood of that entire nation in antiquity, however, would not suffice for fuel for the offering God deserves. The Today's English Version suggests that Lebanon's trees are too few even to "kindle the fire." Furthermore, all the living creatures inhabiting those vast forests are utterly paltry as a burnt offering, altogether unfit to honor *YHWH*.

This verse has profound and painful implications for each of us as individuals and for our churches collectively. What can we learn from the prophet's understated images of the flimsiness of our offerings?

What is the true worship of God? Does God ask us to make sacrifices? Certainly we know that our feeble oblations cannot earn his favor — yet how often do we deceive ourselves, subconsciously assuming that we gain God's grace with our pious efforts?

Though we know better, we Christians are internally torn between the biblical truth that we are saved by God's grace alone through faith, and our frequent (often subconscious) attempts to demonstrate that we're really not so helplessly, hopelessly in need of that grace. We want to please God as a *response* to his love, but instead we find ourselves trying to *prove* our love for him. How hard it is for us truly to receive God's grace as freely as it is given! It hurts our egos to admit that all we are and all we do is made possible by God's action within us and that we can never do anything out of our own abilities to please him.

My husband taught me that in a humorous way. Once in the playfulness of asking "Why do you love me?" I expected him to answer (or hoped he would) with some rapturous exclamation about my gifts or personality or charm. Instead he simply said, "Because you need it."

Blaise Pascal noted in his *Pensées* that the First Testament sacrifices were not sufficient or pleasing to God because at the time they both fulfilled and did not fulfill God's wishes. When the Israelites lost sight of their relationship with their covenant God and resorted instead to meaningless multiplication of sacrifices, their offerings could not fulfill his desire for their love and faithfulness. God's holiness and justice caused him to react with righteous wrath and indignation.

How and when will we learn this truth that instead of burnt offerings God looks for contrite and diligent hearts? Isaiah, Hosea, and many other First Testament prophets emphasize constantly that God is not pleased with empty mechanics. They criticize the people of Israel severely for their hypocritical and phony offerings from the hands and not from the heart (that is, the will). This verse adds the assertion that even the greatest sacrifices (even when offered with true humility and faithfulness) are still puny in comparison with the infinite holiness and transcendent superiority of God. The cosmos is not big enough to be the offering *YHWH* deserves.

Elsewhere the book of Isaiah describes the sacrifices God desires: sacrifices of praise and rejoicing, the heart's gifts of commitment and trust, offerings of justice and compassion. God longs for our very selves, our willingness, devotion, humble submissiveness, faithful obedience, confident dependence, eager witness. He wishes that we would love him with all our heart and soul and mind and strength.

The outcome of that kind of love, of course, is that all the rest of our being is directed properly as well. Then we make the right sacrifices. We do indeed burn up our Lebanons (our very lives) and offer all the animals therein (our gifts and labors). However, the motive is exactly opposite. It is not an attempt to be sufficient; rather, it is the realization that there is no better use of Lebanon or her animals than to offer up our complete selves and service in praise to God.

This gives rise to difficult questions regarding our steward-ship — of our talents and treasures, our time and trust. How do we use our abilities? Do we devote all our skills to making money and a name for ourselves, or do we spend them to fight famine, to secure justice in the world, to support our spouse, to raise godly children, and quietly and reverently to give a defense to those who ask us to account for the hope that lies within us (1 Peter 3:15-16)?

What about our treasures? Do our offerings to our congre-gations buy only organs and stained-glass windows and new shrubs for the landscaping, or are our financial resources being used for the spreading of the Kingdom of God, to offer the narratives of faith to those without a story into which they can place their lives, to feed the hungry, to comfort those without hope? There is nothing wrong with pipe organs; they enhance our worship and lift us to God in incomparable ways. Beautiful furniture, vestments, and other signs and symbols of our adoration are good worship aids, useful assistants for fixing our minds on God. But do our luxurious buildings with all their gorgeous accoutrements become places of pride instead of houses of worship?

Do we realize that any percentage of our income is not enough for our offering? We question whether or not to give a tithe of our income, when God wants 100%. When all our resources are given over to God, we will use it all well for God's purposes in the world. It is hard to justify the way we spend what remains of our income beyond our gifts to our churches when people are starving both physically and spiritually. Is our lifestyle in keeping with the One who called us to sell our possessions and give to the poor?

Sometimes the offering of time is the biggest snare. Lay people are too busy with all the activities our frantic society offers;

professional church workers are tempted simply to put in our time, to do our duties because that is our job. All the animals of Lebanon, all our Bible studies and counseling sessions and council meetings and hospital visitations, are not sufficient to honor the LORD. He wants every moment. How can we practice his presence even when we're not playing our professional parts?

Perhaps all our stewardship can be summed up in the word *trust*. God's desire is for us to surrender all to him and trust his guidance for our way and his provision for our needs. We cannot ever really understand the Atonement, but we know that Jesus' sacrifice of his life and suffering, work and death, was sufficient to reconcile us to God because it was based on a simple trust in the Father's plan for human salvation. Our offerings are a response to Christ's gift of himself when we follow his model of dependent submission.

In the context of the series of rhetorical questions in Isaiah 40 challenging the believer to behold the power and might of God, we can't help but fall humbly to our knees in recognition that we can't even begin to offer anything that is worthy to praise God's imperial name. Only in the confession of our feebleness, only in the realization of the destitution of our sacrifices, can we come humbly into the presence of the omnipotent God and know our proper place before him.

This verse carries us back to the scene of Isaiah 6, wherein Isaiah himself is confronted with the glory and majesty of the Lord GOD, high and lifted up on his throne, with his splendor filling the temple. Isaiah's only response could be the confession, "Woe is me! For I am annihilated; for I am a man of unclean lips." The only response we can make to YHWH's holiness is to recognize our own desperation. Then, when Isaiah had been cleansed, he could commit himself to the LORD's call for someone to go, with the consecration, "Here am I! Send me."

Let us, too, offer the sacrifice of our talents and treasures, our time and our trust — meager tokens of our response to the good news of the LORD's grace. We rejoice with the poet and sing,

> Were the whole realm of nature mine, that were a tribute
>   far too small.
> Love so amazing, so divine, demands my soul, my life, my all!

And let us add, "*Shall have* my soul, my life, my all!"

QUESTIONS FOR FURTHER MEDITATION:

1. How should we understand sacrifice in the Christian faith? What might I be called to offer?

2. What is the value of giving up something for Lent (or similar sacrifices)?

3. To what do I devote my skills and time?

4. How do I make decisions about how to spend my money?

5. How much can I give away for the needs of the world, and how much do I need for myself? How much is enough?

6. How much of the corporate worship service is an offering?

7. What are the strong and weak points of my congregation's "stewardship program"? How could its weak points be strengthened?

17 *The Cry for Biblical Patriotism*

All the nations are as nothing before him;
they are accounted by him as less than
nothing and emptiness.

Isaiah 40:17

I n the last half of the twentieth century it has been hard to keep up with the map of the world. Every year new ethnic squabbles break out, and empires break apart or redivide the territory; new nations are formed, and others are conquered and wiped out of existence. We grieve over the situation of the countless refugees who are being turned away from country after country. Nations fearful of jeopardizing their present political situation consider the refugees people who are good for nothing but trouble.

"Good for nothing," "less than nothing" — these phrases describe what is meaningless, worthless. What a tragedy when human beings are called good for nothing by their families or schoolmates, as was a young woman in the group of camp counselors I've been training this week. We all have to find value in ourselves and believe that we count for others. Yet "less than nothing" is how Isaiah 40 sternly characterizes the nations; this chapter takes us beyond the nations' minuteness, as shown in verse 15, to their complete emptiness in the verse before us now.

"All the nations as not," verse 17 begins literally. The Hebrew word for "not" is the same that was used twice in verse 16, but here it is not followed by the word *enough*. The comparison is significant. Although the forests of Lebanon are not sufficient and her beasts are not adequate to prepare a suitable sacrifice to honor God, there is the implication of at least some value in the phrase "not enough." Here in verse 17, on the other hand, the nations have no value whatsoever. Before the LORD they are "as not."

The extended poetic parallel makes the judgment more severe. It says literally, "They are reckoned to him as less than zero and without form." The verb is the same one used in verse 15, "they are accorded" or "reckoned," although now the phrase "to him" is added. The final word rendered "vanity" or "meaningless" or "emptiness" in various translations is the same Hebrew word that is used in Genesis 1:2 to describe the earth as "without form" and void. Why does the prophet have to go beyond the denunciation of verse 15 to add this oblivion and vanity — or, to use a word from the *Living Bible* paraphrase, "froth"?

Froth on the top of a glass of something is only bubbles, easily blown away, tasting only like air, not providing any substance. In the same way the nations are ephemeral, easily conquered or destroyed, having no meaning, not providing a genuine basis for security or the assurance of a happy life. It is important for us to recognize the totality of their meaninglessness.

This verse is difficult to understand because most of us reading this book live in the most confident nation in the present world. After the breaking apart of the U.S.S.R., the United States stands alone as the superpower, though perhaps not for long. We would more likely rejoice in this verse if we were the people subjected to Babylonian dominion and feeling as if there were no possibility of escape. Only because the nations are nothing in relation to the LORD could Israel be freed from the Babylonian captivity.

It was Babylon especially that Isaiah 40:17 was speaking about — to whittle that world power down to size: nothing. This verse ought to be hard for most of us to read — because now it is the United States that fits the description. Lest we think we're too great because we are the only remaining superpower, let us remember that powerful nations are to God mere froth.

During the era of the U.S. involvement in Vietnam (when I was a teenager), it was the fad among patriots in the United States to have bumper stickers that said, "America: Love It or Leave It!" That slogan insisted that war protesters should make this choice: Either be responsible, as the bumper sticker owners defined responsibility, or give up your citizenship. Those supporting the war demanded that its critics change either their minds or their homeland. Many deep thinking and deeply caring individuals couldn't accept either alternative.

Christians who recognize that this world is not our real home must also wrestle with questions of citizenship. When we love *YHWH* and seek above all to be devoted to him and his purposes in the world, what does it mean to sing "I Love America"? What is a biblical perspective on patriotism?

Loving or leaving the United States — or whatever your homeland is — is not the biblical question. Christians everywhere need to be more radical about issues of citizenship — that is, getting to the root of the matter, thinking critically about the perspective that Isaiah 40 proposes.

Two sets of contrasting experiences on our college choir's mission tour around the world illustrate the main issues that this chapter addresses. The first set is a combination of moments in India and what we then called East Germany.

I'll never forget the Fourth of July that we spent in Vellore,

India. As indicated in Chapter 15, much of our concert tour made me ashamed of my homeland, but Independence Day provided a positive impression. Tears flowed down the cheeks of many of the choir members during the concert when we sang first the Indian national anthem (a custom in every land we visited) and then our own (for the first time on the tour). Then the students of the Christian Medical College set off fireworks to help us celebrate. Women of the choir were dressed in saris for the party, and we had all eaten Indian food for dinner; but the concert had stirred up our love for our homeland, from which we had been absent for a grueling time. That love overflowed for me in thanks to God for all the blessings and the liberty that enabled us to worship God freely. This gratitude was accentuated when, a few weeks later, our choir tried to sing in the Thomaskirke in Leipzig (where J. S. Bach had been the organist and choir master), and our communist guide made us stop. "Es ist verboten," she screamed, and we knew we would never again take for granted the privilege of worship.

The second set of experiences begins with the unexpected burst of joy I felt when I saw the U.S. flag as we flew into an airport in Israel. Amid all the strange experiences and the hostilities we had encountered in our travels, the flag reminded me that at home I felt at home. However, contrary to my expectation at that moment near the Mediterranean, I did not feel at home when we returned to the United States. As we flew into New York City, I remember feeling aghast at all the huge cars and exclusive homes I saw. I could not then — and cannot now — reconcile the materialism and luxury of the United States with the grinding poverty, the famine, and the death that I had witnessed in the Orient and India. Since that first return to the United States, I have never felt at home in my homeland. Our obsessively wealthy culture seems out of joint. The homelessness I experience reminds me that I am made for another world (see Chapter 6).

These are the implications of verse 17 discovered in those two sets of experiences: that nations are nothing before the LORD except as they are with the LORD and that they become meaningless when they contradict our deepest purposes and heritage elsewhere. Both points really are the same.

We Christians so easily become enculturated if the Christian community is not consciously an alternative society. We forget that our national heritage is not our primary birthright. We are above all, as the Scriptures tell us, strangers and aliens. We are sojourners and ambassadors here. It is good to be grateful to the land that is our home. It is good to recognize our nation's strong points and to be thankful for her resources, but it is dangerous to live entirely for the sake of our country. It is absurdity to commit our lives to froth.

It certainly is not wrong to love and serve our country. Yet how easily we make the nation or its people or its weapons of defense our god. One of the most interesting discussions on peacemaking I have ever enjoyed was with a group of Christian military personnel and their spouses, who readily admitted that they continually had to struggle not to misplace their esteem and priorities. They commented on how easy it was to trust their airplanes and bombs instead of God.

Obviously, citizens of the United States presently make a mockery of the nation's original pledge to be "one nation under God." God's sovereignty over our land not only is no longer considered relevant but is more often thought to be an oppressive or hopelessly archaic notion. I believe God is still sovereign over us, but perhaps that might result in his wrath directed at us. Though I am grateful for my country, I cannot give it undivided loyalty. Loving it forces me to be critical of its business tactics and governmental policies, its selling of weapons to feed the world's atrocities, its flagrant practice and exportation of immorality, its exploitation of poorer countries, its consumerism and waste. These certainly cannot be my practices if I am a loving citizen of God's Kingdom.

Augustine fully understood the meaning of verse 17 that nations are as nothing before the LORD when he wrote his famous book *The City of God*. That important work contrasts earthly kingdoms with the heavenly Kingdom and recognizes that Christians are citizens of both at the same time. We dare not become so heavenly minded that we are no earthly good, as the saying goes. God told Israel through Jeremiah to "seek the welfare of the city where I have sent you into exile, and pray to the LORD on its behalf, for in its welfare you will find your welfare" (Jeremiah 29:7). What enables us to be the best possible citizens, however, is our awareness that our primary heritage is our citizenship in a greater Kingdom.

QUESTIONS FOR FURTHER MEDITATION:

1. If nations are meaningless, why should we be concerned about our citizenship in a particular one? Is there a biblical purpose for a nation?

2. How can I distinguish between proper earthly citizenship and a distortion of it?

3. How can I as a Christian best serve our nation? What particular gifts and insights do I have for serving it?

4. How can my citizenship in the Kingdom of God positively contribute to my earthly citizenship?

5. What are the best gifts that my own nation gives for which I am grateful?

6. How can I become more aware of my heavenly citizenship in the mundane affairs of daily life in the earthly sphere?

7. What can I do about the aspects of my homeland that are contrary to the purposes of God? How can I keep from being overwhelmed by them?

18 *The Cry of God's Incomparability*

To whom then will you liken God,
or what likeness compare with him?

Isaiah 40:18

The salesman sprinkled a packet of dirt on my carpet. Then he challenged me to try to pick it up with the ancient vacuum cleaner I was borrowing. After I'd finished, he used his product to go over the same area of floor a few times. When he opened his cleaner's bag, I was astounded at all the dirt we found there. I couldn't deny the evidence. His tool was so very much better that I was glad to pay the extra price to invest in such good equipment.

"It's the real thing!" "Why settle for less?" "I love what you do for me!" "We really know how to fly!" "A fund that outper-formed . . . and a mountain of evidence to prove it." Every adver-tising slogan urges us to compare brands and discover that this one is the best. They imply that we will, of course, recognize the vast superiority of the particular product being touted.

Isaiah 40:18 does somewhat the same thing (although the

chapter's claims about God are obviously infinitely more reliable than marketing endorsements). The prophet asks the penetrating question, "To whom will you liken God?" The form of the question, though, is intensely ironic and, consequently, more piercing.

To create the irony, the poet chooses an unusual word, the name *el*, for God. Usually in the First Testament the plural and elevated form *Elohim* or the name *El* with another name attached (like *Shaddai* — "almighty") is used to designate *YHWH*. Here *el* stands alone as his name.

El was originally the name of the Canaanite chief deity, who seems to have been retired somewhat to a figurehead position with the advent of Baal worship. In the context of this chapter, with its comments about Lebanon, the coastlands (perhaps a reference to the Greek isles, with all their conflicting deities), and the dusty nations, the prophet's choice implies sarcasm. *Elohim* is the real God. To compare anything to the real God reduces him to a mere figurehead, to less than the GOD that he is — in short, to *el*. *YHWH* is the only real God. All the rest are fakes and shams, mere pretenders to the throne.

The irony is reinforced by the verb choice in the poetic parallel, which says, "or what image will you compare to him?" The specific verb rendered "to compare" implies the result of arranging or setting forth, perhaps in battle array against the thing contrasted. The connotation, then, is that those who set false deities in opposition to God discover that no image can stand up in comparison to his power, his sovereignty, all that he is.

This verse serves as a center, a focus in the midst of the fortieth chapter. It helps us to understand all the chapter's rhetorical questions about the magnificence and dominion and immeasurability of God. All the main themes of the chapter evolve from this basic point: Nothing — not flesh, nor idols, nor nations — can compare with *YHWH*.

This verse's significant questions ought also to be the focus

109

of our existence: How can we describe God? By what means shall we come to a greater understanding of *YHWH*? The prophet's challenging sarcasm forces us to realize that the ways we describe God and the false deities that we array against him indicate our minuscule comprehension of his character.

This verse's rebuke of our lives moves in two divergent directions. First, the questions criticize the way we reduce God by making him *el* instead of *Elohim*. (These negative reductions will be considered more thoroughly in the next two chapters.) Second, the verse implies that we should gain a proper perspective on God, and thus it encourages us to formulate rightly our descriptions of him.

On the positive side, this verse urges us to increase our appreciation for all that God is by enlarging our vocabulary about him. The way we perceive *YHWH* affects how we come to him. If we perceive that the name *Father* reduces God to the kind of oppressive, abusing men that many have experienced in their dysfunctional families, we certainly won't turn to him as trusting children. But if we search the Scriptures and discover the totally loving Father that he is — if we picture his gracious sustaining, tender enfolding, and gentle care — we will recognize in him the perfect Father that every human being needs. It is a crucial question, then, "To whom will you liken God?"

Obviously, we cannot compare anyone or anything to God. Nothing comes close to corresponding to him. All our language is inadequate. Even our composite pictures of many, many attributes grouped together only scratch the surface of all God is.

The lifelong challenge before us as believers is continually to explore the nature of God as deeply as we can in order to love and to proclaim that nature more accurately. As much as possible we want to grasp the characteristics by which *YHWH* has made himself known. Certainly we gather for worship and spend time in Bible study and devotional meditation so that we can add and add and add some more to our understanding of what God is like.

The entire quest of theology can be summarized in these two words: "Know God!" Our primary source for doing that is the Bible with all its narratives of God's work in the world and its names for God and descriptions of God's character. The biblical illiteracy in contemporary U.S. culture has resulted in a terribly narrowed picture of God. Some of the biblical pictures we would rather not face — and some of them we overemphasize to the detriment of the dialectical opposites in a true picture of God. For example, our culture likes the coziness of a loving God, but skips over his wrath. We want to feel comfortable with God, but we bypass "the fear of the LORD," which is "the beginning of wisdom." We need all of the Scriptures to reveal to us all that God wants to tell us about himself.

We need four Gospels to give us four different perspectives on the character of Jesus, and still the evangelist John concludes, "But there are also many other things that Jesus did; if every one of them were written down, I suppose that the world itself could not contain the books that would be written" (John 21:25). Furthermore, no matter how many times we study particular sections of the Scriptures, these same passages will continually unlock new truths for us about the nature of God.

Moreover, one of the essential reasons for the Body of Christ is that it takes all of God's people to show us everything God wants to tell us about himself. Consequently, 1 Peter urges us to be good stewards of that which has been given to us, employing our gifts for one another and revealing, by our steward-ship, some of the facets of God's many-sided grace (4:11).

God's grace is so large that even with everyone's contribution we can't begin to fathom its immensity — and that is just one aspect of God's character. We observe elements of his character in many different forms. For example, when first I wrote this chapter I was thinking about an incident that had happened the previous day. My car had stalled on the freeway because my malfunctioning gas gauge indicated I still had ⅜ of a tank, when actually it was nearly empty. I coasted off an exit ramp and reached the bottom of the hill. Not knowing what was wrong, I was quite frightened. Being terribly unmechanical, I had no idea how to begin to figure out what was wrong. However, just when I was about to panic, two young gentlemen stopped, offered to help, pushed until I could get the car started by popping the clutch, and so enabled me to get going again. I was able to travel just far enough to coast finally to a safe place. A friend loaned me her car for the rest of the day until I could get gas for mine.

Those three individuals revealed to me several dimensions of the character of God. That the Father had provided their assistance just at the time of my frantic need was an appropriate picture of how full his provision for us is. That they helped so willingly and so gently, probably sensing both my frustration and my fear, was another picture of God's tender care. I needed to add both pictures to my collage of understanding.

Each day, in all the "ordinaries" of life, we append dimensions of perception to our appreciation for the character of God — always knowing that our cognition is still inadequate. On the day of my first writing of this chapter I saw God's bounty in raspberry fields where he had provided plenty for me, plenty for all the other pickers, and plenty for the birds — with still many left over.

I also saw God's compassion that day as I examined the Bible with a student to explore the subject of death. Together we realized that the Father waits on the other side of death to receive us.

Many things, people, and incidents give us bits and pieces to add to our growing knowledge of the character of God. It's not that they ARE God, but rather that his creatures reveal their Creator. Above all, YHWH is to be found in his Word.

When we try to compare him or describe him or draw an image of him, we find that nothing will do. God cannot be contained. We dare not put him into the box of our favorite, finite portrayal and think that we have comprehended him. Now we merely catch glimpses through his gifts to us. Some day we shall know him face to face, and then, at last, our descriptions will be accurate.

Of course, Isaiah 40 is directing its remarks particularly against the folly of those who make images of God, as we will see in the next verse, but its words force us to admit also the inadequacy of all our perceptions. Surely the more we learn the more we will be stirred to seek after God more diligently. To learn to know God as he has revealed himself to us gives us enough to do for a lifetime, and an eternity besides.

QUESTIONS FOR FURTHER MEDITATION:

1. What are my favorite pictures of God?

2. What images of God would I rather skip over? How else do I make my God too small?

3. What new dimensions of God's character have I learned about in the past few days?

4. What are the primary tools I use to help me learn more about God?

5. How could I train myself to see God more often in the ordinary moments of life?

6. Who is a person who especially teaches me about the character of God?

7. How could my church better serve to expand my understanding of God's character?

19 The Cry against
Beautiful Idolatries

An idol? — A workman casts it,
  and a goldsmith overlays it with gold,
  and casts for it silver chains.

Isaiah 40:19

I was horrified! They had mummified a girl alive to put her inside the Buddha statue. "That is how we give the image a spirit," our guide explained. I learned later that every image of Buddha has the spirit of some creature buried alive inside it, whether it be that of a fly or a person. The craftsman's work is not complete until the spirit is given to his idol.

Such care is taken by a craftsman who makes an idol, who tries to make a god. This verse of Isaiah 40 mocks particularly those who think that God can be compared to something made with hands, something decorated by an artisan. Even though the latter might be overlaid with the most precious of metals, it is still merely constructed.

The humor of this illustration is reinforced by the construction of the Hebrew phrases in this verse. Usually the subject

114

or verb of the sentence comes first; putting the direct object at the beginning, as the poet does here, adds special emphasis. Thus, the first phrase literally reads, "The idol! pours out a craftsman."

The second phrase amplifies the first, stating that "a smith with the gold overlays it." Then the third phrase doesn't have a verb. The word for "smith" is now found in a participial form to convey this extension: "and chains of silver smithing."

The purpose of those chains is unclear. Perhaps they decorate the image. The statement of the following verse, urging that the idol be made skillfully so that it won't totter, might suggest that the chains were used to fasten the image so that it wouldn't fall down. If that is the intent, the last phrase doubly reinforces the irony of the ineffectiveness of human construction. What image could ever be fashioned that could compare with the living God if it needs chains to hold it erect?

I am reminded of conversations with my Taiwanese friend, Yu Chi Ping, who was a Buddhist before becoming a Christian. As a little boy, Chi Ping had watched the idol craftsman make the Buddha — carving it with his tools, giving the statue eyes, shaping its mouth, forming the ears. Then, when his work was completed, Chi Ping's father took the image home, set it up on his altar, and used it for worship. Already as a young person Chi Ping was haunted by this experience. He had observed the making of these idols carved from wood, and yet those idols assumed a prominent place in his home. When I met him in Taipei he had been a Christian for several years, and he told me, still with great enthusiasm, how he had discovered that God is so much larger than an idol, how dedicating his life to Christ filled him with such Joy.

Verse 19 reinforces the criticism of the previous verse, the negative side of which we will consider now in order to allow it to reprimand us. Isaiah 40 was justly sarcastic with the Israelites. To be swept into the worship of the false deities of their neighbors

115

was sheer folly on their part. God had warned them that they must destroy the pagan influences that surrounded them, and he had proved himself time and again to be faithful to his promises and powerful to care for his people. For the Hebrew people to reject such clear evidence was blindly ridiculous.

Lest we condemn them heedlessly, however, let's remember that we all do the same. God has warned us, and he has proved himself faithful time and again — and yet, in blatant rejection or whimpering complaint, we turn away from him to all sorts of false gods. We array against him material pleasures, power and prestige, or the ambitions of the surrounding culture (1 John 2:16's "the lust of the flesh and the lust of the eyes and the pride of life" [RSV]) and never realize how ludicrous is the comparison.

Of course, I don't know what false gods you arrange, but I shudder to recognize how many I set up. How do we reduce God and miss what he wants to be for us and to give to us? When I choose the ease of temptation instead of the struggle of obedience, I miss the ecstasy of victory. When I choose the pleasure of sin instead of the pain of faithfulness, I miss the multifaceted *Shalom* of well-being with God and with myself and with my neighbor. When I crave affirmation from the world to boost my ego, I get hollow accolades that prevent me from hearing the true sense of worth that God confers.

We make so many things into idols without pausing to realize that they are the products of our own hands. We commit our lives to them and invest all our wealth in them. We spend all our time crafting them and all our resources decorating them.

Notice how this verse accentuates the beautiful and thorough work of the idol makers. The first verb actually means "to pour out," so it might suggest the whole process of constructing a mold, refining a metal, and pouring it into the form. Next a smith overlays it with gold, while a silversmith fashions silver

116

chains by which it can hang or be decorated. What idolatries do we spend great effort constructing, hiding the emptiness of our images under an overlay of gold?

When my doctoral dissertation got snagged numerous times for several years in committee problems, I sought a counselor's help for the ensuing depression. He asked me why I needed the degree, and I answered "for credibility." This is not to denigrate the Ph.D., but his next question exposed how I had turned it into an idol. "Why is it always 'Jesus and . . .'?"

At first I didn't understand that question, but he helped me see how often we decorate our idols with a gold overlay of service to God. "I would serve God much more effectively if I just had more money," ". . . if I just had a better congregation to work with," ". . . if I just had more time." What are the "Jesus and's" in your life? I went home that day and listed at least thirty.

So much of what we construct with our own hands — our position or reputation, our books and lectures, our homes and other possessions — is covered with some beautiful veneer to create the illusion of true worth in the service of God. How often does our religious piety mask an idolatry of our own accomplishments or attributes?

Our character and work are God's tools, of course. When we mistake them for ends in themselves, however, and not merely tools for God's service, we add another chain to the idol.

Let me use a trivial example. Because I am the oldest granddaughter on my mother's side, I was given Grandmother's china. Though I try to live simply, I treasure the beautiful china and use it frequently, both as a tie to my heritage and family and also to say to my guests that they are special, that I want to use the best to welcome them to my home.

However, once when a friend was drying a piece, I found myself worrying that he might break it. I was astonished at my feelings — that something humanly made, even though decorated with gold, should become more important than my relationship with a friend.

Our idolatries are more obvious with things like china. Isn't it silly how often we get overly anxious about the things we possess lest anyone damage them, keep them too long, or use them improperly? Of course, we should be good stewards of what God entrusts to us, but we go to ridiculous extremes sometimes in the ways we overlay them with gold in our minds. Another absurd example to make the point: During a visit to me when I was a graduate student and very poor, my brother pointed out that I was disrupting his visit by my overzealous conserving of electricity. How many pennies could I really save by switching off lights the minute he left a room?

The key is remembering the difference between means and ends. Turning off lights is a means to good stewardship, but hardly a goal worth pursuing when spending time with a beloved visitor is the alternative.

We don't buy a house just to own a beautiful house; when it is the end in itself, it has become an idolatry. Rather, we buy a house so that God's purposes for our families might be accomplished and his gift of hospitality extended.

Sometimes our very church buildings are turned into ends. We worry about their fine furnishings too much if we are reluctant to let outsiders from the community use the facilities for ministering efforts, such as meetings of Alcoholics Anonymous or a day-care center for senior citizens. Do our churches or professions or accomplishments entice us to worship them, or do they aid us in serving and focusing our attention on God?

The understanding of idolatries does not mean the elimination of possessions or the ending of pleasures. We must remember, however, that such things are never ends in themselves. Our pleasures and possessions, our positions and professions are means to the end of loving God and glorifying him forever. When everything we use and have and do is understood as a gift on loan from God, we break the silver chains by which our idols are hung.

QUESTIONS FOR FURTHER MEDITATION:

1. What are some possessions that I have made into idols?

2. What are some accomplishments or personal attributes that I have made into idols?

3. What gold overlays do I use to hide my idolatries from myself?

4. How can I be a successful image breaker without losing sight of those things that God gives me to enjoy and of which I could be a good steward?

5. How can I faithfully use things to grow in my appreciation of God, without beginning to worship those things themselves?

6. How can I enjoy God's creation without having to possess it unjustly?

7. What idolatries have invaded my congregation?

20 *The Cry against Idolatries of Security*

The one too impoverished for [such] an offering
  selects a tree that does not rot,
then seeks out a skilled artisan
  to establish an idol that will not totter.

Isaiah 40:20 (composite)

Y ou can't win either way. If someone asks in jest, "Have you stopped beating your child?" either answer gets you in trouble.

Isaiah 40 sets up the same sort of dilemma from which there is no escape in verse 20. The prophet intends to force the Israelites to confront the irrationality of their dependence on idols.

You can't win either way. You want to construct the idol securely enough so that it won't topple. But making it that secure reinforces the realization that this god can't move at all to help you. What is the value of a non-tottering image?

Once again the irony of the situation emerges forcefully as Isaiah 40 continues to describe human efforts to make idols. The prophet's anguish over all the misdirected effort is poignantly

120

apparent. First, he contrasts those "too impoverished for a contribution" with the wealthy ones who could purchase the idols overlaid with gold and hung with silver (v. 19). (Though the Hebrew is not clear in this verse, I think this interpretation is more likely than the translation of the NRSV, "as a gift one chooses mulberry wood.") Although the poor cannot lavish such attention and money on their images, the prophet notes that they do their best. At least they are careful when they select their tree so that their idol is made of wood that will not rot. They do everything they can to make the idol last, but even the best wood cannot last forever. Ultimately it, too, withers as the grass (verses 6-8).

Next, the poor choose a skillful artisan, one who has the ability and technique to carve a fitting image. Above all, they want the craftsman to construct the idol so that it "shall not be moved" (KJV), a "sturdy image" (JB) that "will not topple" (NRSV).

The irony is doubly reinforced in this last phrase by two word choices. To describe the action of the artisan in constructing the idol, the prophet chooses a verb that is used in the First Testament to describe the "establishing" of kings, or the heavens, or anything else by the faithfulness of God. The craftsman seeks to establish the idol as firmly as God fixed the mountains. This effort is further accentuated by the final word choice of the verse, which stresses that the impoverished ones and their artisans want an idol that will not be shaken or moved, even if they can't afford the silver chains to secure it. Artisan and worshiper alike require a firm idol that won't tumble, that nothing can knock over. How vastly different it is when one's God is the One who himself established everything and yet is swayed by our needs. *YHWH* stands in stark contrast to the result of our efforts to establish gods that cannot move or be moved.

Pondering this verse, I am reminded of our choir's visit to the largest Buddha in central Taiwan. Precaution was taken to protect the Buddha by various entrance monsters. As I observed the Buddha and the people praying, I kept hearing in my mind the words from Psalm 115:4-8 concerning idols that have ears but do not hear, that have mouths but cannot speak. There was the Buddha, a huge iron hulk, unable to do anything for the despairing people who prostrated themselves before it, except to model for them the original Gautama's ability not to be moved by his own life's situations. This image's hands could not reach out to heal or to comfort.

Having discovered that it was possible to go up inside the Buddha's head, I climbed to the top and looked out through the eyes. From that perspective I was profoundly saddened by the seemingly fatalistic attitude of the worshiping peasants. Chi Ping had told me how he had felt that he had little basis for hope, and this image could not give him any. No matter how skillful the work of the artisan, his image could not change Chi Ping's life.

In this chapter we focus on idolatries of security, though of course these often turn out to be the same as our idolatries of confusing means with ends. The accent here is on the things or events or circumstances we trust for protection. No matter how carefully we choose and establish what will keep us safe, our gods lead only to futility and meaninglessness. The idol cannot move.

Sometimes we don't even pretend to overlay our idols with gold, but instead, out of our impoverishment, we clutch frantically at anything that seems dependable. We grasp for some sort of god to sustain us in the crises of our lives, to withstand the rapid changes in our culture, to keep us safe until we die. How much money is enough to last us, how much power will keep us important, how many business contacts will assure us that we can maintain our lifestyle?

What god can weather the stock market crashes or the book failures? What god can make sure that people we love will survive with us into old age? What god can keep our homes from fire or theft? What god will ease the longing of the *Sehnsucht* (see

Chapter 6) deep within us? Sometimes we even make false gods out of the securities of our worship.

When I first wrote this book, I was facing a change of work that necessitated a move to another city. It was shocking to me how terribly insecure I felt moving out of the office at the parish I'd been serving for more than three years and not knowing to what I was moving. It is astonishing for me now to realize how easily a home or office or position can become a god, and how desperately we need it not to totter. Something — anything! — must be secure when everything else around a person seems to be shifting.

A final point to note is the totality of our failure and incapability when we consider this verse in relation to its context. We see the futility of our humanly made gods (verses 18-20), the inadequacy of the offerings we bring (verse 16), the pretensions of our nationalistic pride (verses 15 and 17). Above all, we recognize our rebellions against God as we crave other securities and purposes in life.

Into that failure and incapability comes the grace of Jesus Christ. We don't need a skilled artisan; we don't need to overlay our own creations with a veneer of gold; we don't need chains to keep our god erect. Instead, we believe that *YHWH*, THE Skillful Craftsman, has given us the uncreated image of himself, the One begotten but not made, who offers himself as the Offering. When we rest in the Christ, who sacrificed himself, and thereby know the Father by the Spirit's power, only then are offering and God successfully brought together.

QUESTIONS FOR FURTHER MEDITATION:

1. For what reasons do I turn to other gods in the first place?
2. To what do I turn for security?

3. *What kinds of skilled craftsmen, such as advertisers, set up idols to which I turn?*

4. *How have I experienced the inadequacy of the gods I create?*

5. *Does the Bible overstate the case about our helplessness?*

6. *What prevents us from thoroughly experiencing our total inadequacy and incapability without God?*

7. *What sorts of things prevent people from turning away from their false gods? How could I be helpful in leading people away from gods that can't move or be moved?*

21 *The Cry to Know and Hear*

Have you not known? Have you not heard?
  Has it not been told you from the beginning?
  Have you not understood from the foundations of the earth?
                                                    Isaiah 40:21

Why couldn't she remember where to stand on the volleyball court? I had told her so many times how to figure out where her position should be when the opponents were serving, and yet we consistently lost points because she wasn't in place to return the serve. She should have been able to deduce her place just by noticing everyone else's position on the court. And we'd been telling her about the formations ever since she first started playing with us. She ought to have understood by now! Hadn't she been listening?

The prophet also wonders if anyone has been listening as he asks a painful set of questions with a tone of exasperated impatience. Isaiah 40 challenges us to realize that we ought to know better, that we should have paid better attention when we could have heard, that we might have been listening more when things were first told us at the beginning, that we could have understood from the very fact of creation itself. We have no excuse.

Each phrase in this verse begins with a form that combines the interrogative with a word that means "not." Thus, the verse keeps saying, "Do you not?" "Do you not?" as if to ask, "Well, why don't you?"

The first verb form is one of continuous action in the Hebrew. It asks, "Will you not know?" or "Are you not yet knowing?" as if to say, "Have you not figured it out yet so that you keep on not knowing?" The verb root is a repetition of the one that occurs in both verses 13 and 14 and again in 14 as a noun. Such frequent repetition in those verses to state that no one can help God to know contrasts sharply with the painful point here that human beings do not yet know the truth.

"Will you not hear?" Isaiah 40 continues. The phrase reminds us of the original message given to the prophet Isaiah when he first received the sublime vision of *YHWH* and responded with readiness to be sent (Isaiah 6). God told him to proclaim to the people, "Hearing, do not hear" (6:9). The people's ears were dulled by their own rebellion. Again, the verb here is in an imperfect, or not-yet-completed form. The question might be rendered, "Have you not yet come to hear?" or "Are you still not hearing?"

The third question of this verse asks in the Hebrew, "Has it not been told you from the head?" — from the beginning, the first, the source. God, who is the Beginning, has revealed himself from the start. In fact, as the final question asserts, we should have understood from the "foundations of the earth."

Throughout the history of the Church, theologians have argued over whether there is such a thing as natural revelation in addition to God's disclosure of himself in his Word. This verse combines the two. First it suggests that something of God can be surmised from the foundations of the earth. Then *YHWH's* specific revelation of his character is implied by the phrase, "Has it not been told you from the beginning?" God's character is displayed both in what we observe and in what he has told us through his Word.

The four questions of this verse are not mere rhetoric. They are terribly indicting. Are we so ignorant? Why are we so deaf to the words of God? Why can't we comprehend God's speech? Can't we grasp what has been going on for a long time? It has been declared for us; why haven't we perceived it?

Jesus reiterates the prophet's indictment in Mark 8. After two instances of feeding the multitudes (first the 5,000 men plus women and children and then the 4,000 plus), followed each time by discussion with the Pharisees and then the specific healing of an individual, Jesus asks the disciples who the world says that he is. When they respond, "John or Elijah," he asks them what they think. Peter's confession, "You are the Christ," is the climax of Mark's entire narrative. Yet just prior to this conversation the disciples had been with Jesus in the boat. Worrying that they had no bread, they misunderstood Jesus' warning to them to avoid the leaven of the Pharisees.

Jesus rebukes them in words reminiscent of Isaiah 40. Piercingly, he questions them, "Do you still not perceive or understand? Are your hearts hardened? Do you have eyes, and fail to see? Do you have ears, and fail to hear? And do you not remember? . . . Do you not yet understand?" (Mark 8:17-18, 21).

Prefacing Peter's declaration, "You are the Christ," these questions rebuked the disciples for failing to learn who Jesus was and is. Even after making this glorious proclamation, Peter himself did not understand and tried to talk Jesus out of his mission as the Christ to die (Mark 8:31-33).

These questions are even more critical now in our postmodern world. Postmodern philosophers insist that there is no truth to be known and that all of our ways of knowing are simply battles for power. Every person has unique ways of seeing and hearing, and there is no common means by which we could agree on anything without that being oppressive. Any meaning that exists in the world is what you create for yourself on the basis of opinions and feelings.

Against the vagrant solitariness of these attitudes, Christianity offers a refreshing alternative. There is a community that has carried on a relationship with God over the centuries since Abraham. The Truth that this people has passed on is not in itself oppressive, though it has often been passed on in oppressive ways. It is the Truth of a God whose promises have always been kept, of a grace that sets us free instead of oppressing us, of a love that enables us to be truly ourselves.

Why don't we understand? We don't know or hear or understand because we're not part of a community that passes on the faith. Our churches forget why they exist and become battlegrounds for power or venues of personal pride or "charisma" instead of genuine communities that nurture Christian faith.

One of the biggest obstructions is our simple neglect of the means God has given us for growth in our awareness, renewal in our mind. The LORD of the cosmos has given us his Word, and he told us that it alone stands forever. Yet we fail to read it, to study it, to meditate upon it, to "hide it in our hearts."

When first I was writing this book, we had been conducting an experiment for more than a year in the congregation that I served. The project stressed discipleship and involved eighteen other persons who met with me in three groups, who diligently sought to make use of the opportunities God makes available for us to grow in our faith. This led to a valuable struggle.

We met weekly to establish and improve our habits of corporate worship, personal Bible meditation, and prayer. As a group we studied and prayed together, discussed our troubles, and held each other accountable. We ran into all kinds of obstructions and became aware that all kinds of powers of evil work against our growth in being God's people. Sometimes we encountered obstacles from the inside — little hurts or bad attitudes, nagging guilts or petty pride — that had not been dealt with graciously. Sometimes we had to surmount obstacles from the outside — people's criticism or mockery, strains on our time, pressures from work — in order to have the freedom to hear and understand.

Not only is it rare for churches to provide such opportunities for extended hearing and understanding of the Word, but many congregations are even sacrificing their own identity as a people possessing the Truth in their worship services. Instead of offering more truth to our confused world, numerous churches in which I've worshiped throughout the United States have few Bible studies, unbiblical sermons, songs that do little or nothing to form the character, youth groups that are only fun and games.

If we as God's people have not known, perhaps we have never been taught. If we have not heard, maybe it is because we have not taken advantage of opportunities to hear the Word of God being spoken. Above all, God desires to reveal himself to all people. We fail to trust him for his revelation because we do not yet understand that he is such a God of grace.

What do we do, then, with the indictments of this verse? We can react in one of two ways — one from the law and the other from the gospel. If we take this verse only as a word of law, it is an injunction saying to us, "Shape up or ship out." If we can't manage sufficiently well this process of understanding, we might as well forget it and give up.

On the other hand, we can hear this Word as a message of gracious invitation, even though it is indicting. This indicting Word becomes, then, a Word of hope for us nonetheless. We have failed to hear and understand and know, but God's Word to us is forgiveness and not condemnation. He does not come to us with wrathful judgment against our ignorance and neglect. He comes to us through the reconciling work of Jesus and invites us to change that situation, beginning now. These words can serve as an inspiration to us to accept his forgiveness and grace and to let them free us to begin to know better, to pay more attention, to listen, to see.

God does indeed want to reveal himself to us more deeply; if we're not growing in our knowledge of him, it is never because he has not made such growth possible. If we fail to perceive his grace and to learn of his character, it is because we have passed over spending time with him. (Even if what we learn at times is truth about the hiddenness of God, that increases our comprehension of his infinite mystery.) What better motivation can there be for us to establish habits of quiet time and study and worship?

It IS possible for us to know. It IS achievable for us to hear. Good news HAS been declared to us from the beginning. We WILL be able to understand — by the grace of God. It's a matter of opening our eyes, ears, hearts, and minds — and Bibles.

QUESTIONS FOR FURTHER MEDITATION:

1. What means might I use to become better acquainted with the revelation of God?

2. How can I grow in my ability to listen when God speaks and to understand what he says?

3. How can I apply these words to myself as invitation and not condemnation?

4. How can I make the knowledge of God a knowledge of the heart (that is, the will) as well as of the head?

5. What do I do about passages in the Scriptures or revelations from God that I just can't understand?

6. What is it exactly that I am supposed to know, hear, and understand?

7. Why is this verse important in my relationships with others?

22 *The Cry of God's Dwelling*

It is he who sits above the circle of the earth,
and its inhabitants are like grasshoppers;
who stretches out the heavens like a curtain,
and spreads them like a tent to live in.

Isaiah 40:22

I don't know how to pitch a tent, have never done it, and would certainly make a mess of it if I tried. The Bedouins of the Middle East, on the other hand, set up their tents with ease. They have lived in them all their lives, traveling from one place to another according to the seasons and work. To spread out a tent is for them a very simple operation.

Just as easily as the Bedouins, Isaiah 40 proclaims, *YHWH* spreads out the heavens. After the prophet's mockery of the idol makers and his rebuke of those who should know but have not heard and do not understand, the prophet returns to his theme of the majesty and sovereignty of God. Again he compares God to human beings and notes the discrepancy.

The verse revolves around the theme of dwelling. The

Hebrew term occurs twice in the first two lines as a participle, the first time in a singular form referring to God's "dwelling upon the vault of the earth." The second time it is plural to identify "[the earth's] dwelling ones," who are, in comparison to God, "like grasshoppers." God's sovereignty is imagined by his dwelling above the dome of the earth's sky — his reigning majestically from the throne of the heavens. In stark contrast, those dwelling under that dome are as grasshoppers — small, insignificant, noisy, perhaps even pesky.

Finally, the Hebrew root for dwelling occurs again as an infinitive in the last poetic couplet, when the prophet describes God as "stretching the heavens out like a curtain and spreading them out like a tent to dwell in." The word translated "tent" in the last phrase signifies a normal Bedouin tent, used from before the time of Abraham and still observable in the Middle East today.

Once again, anthropomorphic images merely hint at the infinity of God. The first set of parallel lines continues the theme of God's greatness introduced earlier in Isaiah 40. The pictures suggest God's providential upholding and maintaining of the universe. They give us another glimpse of his sovereign care. We look up at the wide expanse of sky and realize that *YHWH* is LORD of the cosmos.

Let us pause to consider how extraordinarily crucial the earth's atmosphere is. We all know that it is the "vault of heaven" that enables life to exist as it does on planet earth. We all know how the destruction of the ozone layer threatens creatures and land and human beings. Stop to think how amazing it is that the earth's temperature range is appropriate for life, that the amount of moisture is sufficient, that earth hasn't collided lately with major meteors. The wonder of life preserved on earth reveals to us a God sovereign over the universe.

Long ago I saw a "Twilight Zone" television episode in which many of the people of the world were moving north because the planet was getting so hot. According to the story, the earth was wandering out of its normal course and growing constantly closer to the sun. As people in the fable conversed, some said they were leaving soon for the north, while others wondered if it was worth the effort. Soon the North Pole, too, would be too hot to survive.

After agonizing scenes of thirsty, frying people throughout almost the entire length of the program, the girl who had been the central figure awoke from sleep and saw that it was snowing outside. All of this terror had been a dream. She exclaimed to the doctor attending her, "How wonderful it is to see the snow! It feels so good to be cold!" After she returned to sleep and the doctor moved away from her bedside, he asked another member of the family if she was planning to move south to escape the growing cold. Actually what was happening was that the earth was moving *away* from the sun!

Although I saw that episode more than thirty years ago, it is indelibly planted in my mind. As a child, I learned from it great gratitude for the fact that GOD sits enthroned above the vault of the earth. I knew with deep thanks that he is the One who uses gravity and the interactions of planets to keep the globe in its place and allows the sun's distance to be just right so that earth can survive.

That is the kind of graciously sovereign God we have. In stark contrast, we must realize that we are much less than grasshoppers. Even subatomic particles are not small enough to describe our insignificance compared to the One who sits enthroned above the earth's vault. As the new physics and astronomy search for explanations for the earth, this verse from Isaiah 40 gives us perspective. I always find it amusing when scientific reports end by listing all the new questions that have been raised by the reported research. There will *always* be new mysteries to explore, for our minds and understandings are like an ant's in comparison with the creative wisdom and sustaining might of the LORD of the cosmos. No matter how much the sciences discover about the "how," the Bible will still tell us the "Who." We cannot but gasp with wonder as we begin to comprehend the intricate interrelationships and colossal macro- and micro-dimensions of God's unfathomable universes.

The second set of parallel lines in verse 22 presents a homey picture of God's stretching out the heavens as a curtain or a tent. I love choosing fabrics and colors for floors and walls and fixing up curtains when I move into a new home. Again Isaiah 40 uses a graphic image to hint at God's magnificence. It is astounding to try to imagine the vast dimensions of the curtains God hangs. We measure in hundreds of miles the firmament that God hangs as easily as we suspend drapes on a rod. He chooses sublime colors for his curtains and even changes them myriads of times each day.

The parallel picture suggests his spreading the heavens like a tent in which to dwell. That illustration is especially precious because it anticipates his future dwelling among us and describes his presence among us now.

The word *tent* and the theme of "dwelling" are important throughout both the First and Second Testaments. The presence of God "tabernacling" himself among us forms a thread throughout the history of God's people. This theme begins in the book of Exodus, when God gives specific instructions for his people to construct the tabernacle in which he will dwell. After several chapters of instructions, several more chapters detail the completion of the tabernacle's fabrication. Finally in Exodus 40, the most glorious event occurs: God comes to dwell in that tabernacle. As his overwhelming glory descends upon the tent, the people rejoice, for no one can doubt that *YHWH* has come and filled the tabernacle with his radiating presence. He fills it so completely that no one can even enter. Glory pulsates from the tent of his presence.

The terrible tragedy in the book of Ezekiel is that this presence departs. Slowly, magisterially, the glory of *YHWH* rises and moves out from the holy place. Hope seems to be crushed forever when it departs from the city of Jerusalem, although it returns again at the end of the book.

The image of dwelling is picked up again in the Gospel of John, when the beloved evangelist writes that the Word became flesh and "tabernacled" himself among us (1:14). Jesus actually pitched his tent among human beings to dwell with them to reveal the grace and truth of God.

The book of Revelation anticipates God's final tabernacling. God declares that he, the Alpha and the Omega, the Beginning and the End, will make his dwelling with human beings. Both noun and verb forms of the word for tabernacling are used in Revelation 21 to proclaim that someday God will again "pitch his tent" among us, for he is our God, and we are his people.

Most important, in 2 Corinthians 12:9 Paul chooses the same verb to proclaim why he can glory in his suffering. He has talked about his thorn in the flesh and about the grace of God that is sufficient for him. Then he declares, literally, "I shall all the more glory in my weaknesses that the power of God may tabernacle in me." When God tabernacles himself in us, his grace is all we need. And the point at which he can tabernacle most easily and thoroughly is when we recognize our weakness and invite him in to dwell. When our power is brought to its end, then his power can flow through us to conform us to his image.

Right now we experience the LORD's tabernacling in our weakness. In our presumption to know the cosmos without God, human beings miss God's tabernacling. If we by faith know his dwelling in our lives now (see John 14:23), we are more likely to recognize that it was God who spread the heavens to be his dwelling place — no matter how he did it.

Together, the two sets of parallel phrases in this verse

135

present wonderful images of God's transcendent preeminence. God is not only a great God beside whom we are less than grasshoppers but also a God who establishes the endless galaxies to dwell in. Yet that same infinitely unfathomed God comes into space and time to dwell with us in all the grace and truth of Christ. Someday *YHWH* will pitch his tent with us forever, and then all his transcendence and immanence will be one.

QUESTIONS FOR FURTHER MEDITATION:

1. *With what other pictures can I describe God's enthronement over the cosmos?*

2. *What other scientific facts, besides the proper distance between the earth and the sun, accentuate the precision of God's sovereign care over the vault of the earth?*

3. *What is the value of recognizing my "grasshopperishness"?*

4. *What feelings are conveyed to me by the figure of God stretching out the heavens like a curtain?*

5. *What other places in the Scriptures emphasize the theme of God's dwelling with his people?*

6. *How can I experience more thoroughly God's tabernacling in my own life?*

7. *How does it help me now to know that in the future God will personally tabernacle among human beings?*

23 *The Cry against Political Illusions*

[He it is] who reduces rulers to nothing,
who makes the judges of the earth meaningless.

Isaiah 40:23 (NAS)

Only in the fairy tales do princes live happily ever after. We have all seen that the princes and rulers of this world get deposed, don't get reelected, or can't persuade the legislature to go along with their plans. Every ruler has at least a few enemies. None can satisfy every demand.

In fact, Isaiah 40 adds, it is the LORD who deposes the world's rulers. Literally, the Hebrew phrase describes God as the one "giving the princes to not," and the word for "not" is the same one we encountered in verses 16 and 17.

That God reduces the world's princes to nothing is understood by a sort of joke in the Hebrew. The word in the first line that we translate as "princes" comes from a verb root meaning "to be weighty" or "to be commanding." Even as the nations are "not" in verse 17, so the LORD reduces the weighty rulers to the absence of weight.

137

The poetic parallel utilizes another striking word that we have encountered previously. The line "and judges of the earth as emptiness he makes" stresses again the meaninglessness of being "without form" that we observed in verse 17 and Genesis 1:2. The same vacuum that characterized the nations and the cosmos before creation is now shown also to be the truth about the world's governors and lawgivers.

This verse moves us from the dwellers of the earth in general in the previous verse to the earth's leaders in particular. Prestige and fame, influence and glory are brought to naught by the LORD. Powers and kingdoms eventually fall.

These comments had a double significance for those first hearing this verse. They rebuked any rulers of Israel who were unduly proud or falsely confident in their divine chosenness. And this verse also spoke about the rulers of the nations that threatened Israel. The Babylonian princes might appear to have power, but they, too, were nothing in *YHWH's* hands. He allowed them to chastise his people, but even the great Cyrus fulfilled God's prophecies in allowing the remnant to return from the Babylonian captivity.

Still today — though we hardly realize it — God brings princes to naught, for the LORD and his justice will ultimately prevail. This message has international, national, and personal consequences.

When I first wrote this book many years ago, my comments about the international implications of this verse were prophetic. I wrote that Christians need not fear those rulers who intended to eliminate Christianity. I remember the occasions when communist leaders swore that they would wipe out the free world and bring it to nothing. I insisted that we didn't have to fear statements like that if we believed God is sovereignly in control and would not allow his people to be totally defeated. At the time I first wrote I mentioned Khrushchev, the Soviet leader who beat

138

his shoe on the table and vowed U.S. annihilation, who was later quietly removed from power and dropped from the memory of the Soviet world. Now, however, we have witnessed the disintegration of the Soviet system and the resurgence of Christianity in formerly atheistic lands.

The Hebrew prophets provide a longer historical example of God's fulfillment of his promises to care, of *YHWH's* covenant with the chosen people. Although they were a nation of little account, and although they were conquered by mighty princes and taken into captivity time and again, yet a remnant always returned. Those mighty rulers themselves (Nebuchadnezzar, Hitler) have long since been destroyed and cut down from their positions of power, whereas many Jewish people continue to believe in *YHWH,* their covenant God of promise.

Nationally, this verse carries a painful reminder and a warning, especially at the time of this rewriting. In U.S. politics in recent years there have been too many examples of government officials who have sought power with deceptive and immoral means. Watergate and Senate ethics hearings have brought their leadership down. This verse warns our present governmental leaders to remember the importance of morality, to realize constantly that the power of earthly authority is vanity.

Most important, however, we must each apply this verse honestly to our own lives. It speaks directly to all our political illusions. Jacques Ellul's book, *The Political Illusion,* rebukes Christians for forgetting the lordship of Christ and thinking that if we just elect the right governmental leaders all our problems will be solved. All earthly officers are sinful human beings. They will fail; some will fall. We cannot place our hopes on a particular political party or program. Human problems are greater than that.

Moreover, verse 23 speaks to the issue of the lordship of our own lives. Does God reign in how we spend our money and time? Do we live out of power or servanthood? If God is really going to be LORD in our lives, WE can't be. If Jesus is really King, we cannot be antagonistic princes or princesses trying to usurp the throne.

Long ago we frequently sang at our Bible study gatherings a song called "Reign, Master Jesus, Reign." Each time we sang it, I was forced to ask myself if I was really serious about it. Do I really want Jesus to be master over everything?

Martin Luther's great insight, recorded in his treatise "Advice to the German Nobility," was that a Christian is slave of none and master of all; and yet, paradoxically, he is slave to all and master of none. In other words, Christians are so free from the rule of others that we can willingly submit to them. We are not governed by them, but therefore can choose to serve them.

If we thoroughly learn that the LORD brings princes to naught, we will be more willing to forego our attempts to assert power over others. Instead, we will want to ask Christ to reign in our lives wherever that might take us, whatever that might cause us to do, however that might lead us to suffering. I think, for example, of the courageous Christian king of Norway, Haaken VII, and of the Norwegian school teachers and church leaders who refused to submit to Hitler's demands and paid a heavy price for declining to train others in an ideology inimical to the Kingdom of God.

Do we want to make that kind of commitment? Are we seriously willing to serve no matter what the cost? Are we able to give up our rights?

Clamoring for rights is the national pastime these days, it seems. Many years ago I agreed with many of the goals of the women's liberation movement — especially that women should be allowed to use their gifts responsibly for the benefit of society. But I still disagree with an insistence upon rights without attendant concern for responsibilities. Women cannot claim a moral "right to their bodies" in abortion when they have been irresponsible in their genital involvement.[1] Similarly, we don't have any authentic right to welfare if we are not willing to use our abilities for the sake of others (see 2 Thessalonians 3:10-13). There must be justice in the world, and Christians should be first in the world to help build it.

We can't clamor for rights and still obey Christ's model and instruction to be the servants of all (Mark 10:42-45). If we really want the Trinity to be the master in our lives, we must listen to these words of Paul: "Let the same mind be in you that was in Christ Jesus, who, though he was in the form of God, did not regard equality with God as something to be exploited, but emptied himself, taking the form of a slave" (Philippians 2:5-7a). Christ is the supreme model of humility and submission, of giving up rights for the sake of God's purposes.

Our leadership is never based on power that withers or fame that fades. As servants, instead, we will grow more and more willing for God to bring our power to naught so that he might be glorified through us. What really matters in life are the eternal things, and eternal values have little or nothing to do with earthly accomplishments. This certainly does not mean that we accept mediocrity from ourselves in leadership. Choosing to be servants who glorify God causes us to strive after excellence, to serve with the best of our abilities. But if we are willing to let the LORD be our God, he creates our worth and value — eternally. Then our importance does not fade with the passing of time.

This spirit was so admirably demonstrated by John the Baptizer when his disciples objected that Jesus was baptizing more than he. John replied, "He must increase, but I must decrease" (John 3:30). The Christian Church year honors that spirit by

1. See chapter 13 on "Abortion" in Marva J. Dawn, *Sexual Character: Beyond Technique to Intimacy* (Grand Rapids: Wm. B. Eerdmans, 1993), pp. 146-50, in the context of the book's wholistic presentation of sexuality.

placing Christ's birth in the season when sun time begins to increase in the northern hemisphere (the early Roman calendar was off by a few days on the solstices) and John's birthday on June 24, when sun time begins to decrease. The more we want to live to the glory of God, the more we will desire his presence in our lives to increase and our selfish egos to decrease.

That is not to say that we won't be fulfilled in our lives. In fact, the paradoxical truth is that we will be far more deeply satisfied. We will be otherwise directed; we will not seek after gratifying our own desires, but we will seek to meet the needs of others. Devoting our lives to greater ends than our own happinesses by serving to benefit those around us, we will discover that true happiness is a by-product, not to be found when we are looking for it, but to be received as a gift when we give ourselves totally to the Creator of all Joy.

It is God's grace that the LORD brings our attempts at importance to naught. Then he can confer upon us the greatest significance of all, his rule in our lives.

QUESTIONS FOR FURTHER MEDITATION:

1. How have I seen in history that princes and governors are brought to naught?

2. What areas of my life are not yet really under the lordship of Christ?

3. How would it change Christian leadership if we all understood ourselves primarily as servants?

4. How can I assist Christian leaders in recognizing the truth of this verse and its application to their lives?

5. How can I strive after excellence without elevating my ego?

6. What are some of the attributes of being a servant after the pattern of Christ?

7. What will help me to grow in a spirit of servanthood?

24 *The Cry of Temporality*

Scarcely are they planted, scarcely sown,
scarcely has their stem taken root in the earth,
when he blows upon them, and they wither,
and the tempest carries them off like stubble.

Isaiah 40:24

There is a huge difference between the way my husband gardens and the way I would. Two words summarize all the contrasts between his horticulture and mine: His grows! Myron supplies us with plenty of vegetables and berries. His flowers surround our home from February till November, and his tropical trees grace the patio in summer. He takes care of all the indoor plants; I know too well what would happen if I did it. Flower seeds I was given once long ago when I was an English teacher germinated after I planted them, but then toppled over only a few weeks later. Scarcely had they taken root when they withered away.

That is the way Isaiah 40 describes the princes of the earth. "Yea," verse 24 begins, with an impassioned rhetorical word in Hebrew that denotes the addition of something even greater than was just said in the last verse. Then a negative particle at the beginning of each of the next three phrases expresses an action hardly even commenced.

"Yea, scarcely shall they be planted, scarcely shall they be sown, scarcely rooted in the earth their stalk — until he shall blow upon them." The last of these three events is in a participial form, which connects it more closely to the following comment and which seems to imply that the plants' taking root might not even quite have happened.

Then, when the LORD blows upon them, "they shall dry up." Both of these verbs about the blowing and the drying are repetitions of the word choices in verses 7 and 8. Consequently, they bring to our minds the comments there about all flesh being grass. This time, however, the prophet adds that "the whirlwind as stubble shall lift them up." The verb in this last phrase is also a repetition of one occurring earlier. In both verses 4 and 11, this word is used in a positive sense to speak of the exalting of the valleys and of the shepherd's carrying of the lambs. Here, negatively, the world's rulers are lifted up by the storms of world affairs as easily as if they were straw.

This verse attaches several significant dimensions to the emphasis on impermanence in previous verses (especially verses 6-8). Here the stress is placed on the relationship between the temporality of the planting and the finality of the carrying away. Rulers and lawmakers trusting in their own machinations and power might think they are firmly rooted, but the LORD's blowing upon them proves them wrong. The domination of flesh cannot be firmly rooted. The whirlwinds and the LORD's blowing just accentuate the inherent problem that the plants are not thriving because they are only straw.

In contrast, those who depend on the power of God and not their flesh can be firmly planted, as many images of the New Testament show. The letter to the Ephesians includes a prayer that they might become so rooted and grounded in Christ's love that they will know its length and breadth and depth and height (3:17-18).

Similarly, the epistle to the Colossians encourages the people that, just as they trusted Christ for salvation, so they might also trust him for each day's problems, that rooted and grounded in him they might grow up to know the fullness of his provision for their needs (2:6-7). These prayers remind us that there is no danger of being blown away when we are rooted in Christ.

We might carry the comparison of my husband's gardening to mine a bit further here. His plants do so much better because he continues to care for them diligently and wisely. Just so, the rooting and grounding of the Church depend on careful nurturing. Jesus, of course, uses the image of rooting in his parable of the sower. Those seeds that fell among the stones sprang up quickly without depth and consequently were scorched and withered away (Matthew 13:5-6). In our essentially superficial and entertainment-centered culture, the Christian community especially needs to be an alternative society offering the narratives of faith clearly and profoundly to root people in the ongoing belief-formed life of God's people.

The last phrase of Isaiah 40:24 — that the whirlwind carries them away like chaff — is analogous to both the seed planted in the path and that which fell among thorns in Jesus' parable (Matthew 13:4, 7). In these cases we are either carried away by powers of evil or choked out by the cares and temptations of the world. Both have the effect of a whirlwind on strawlike faith.

The conclusion of Jesus' parable gives us the positive hope for this verse from Isaiah 40. Rather than being carried away or dried up because we have not been adequately planted, the people of God provide the milieu in which the seed — the Word of God, Jesus says — falls on good soil and bears fruit (Matthew 13:8). The Christian community prepares the earth so that its members

145

can be rooted and grounded in Christ, as we read in Ephesians and Colossians.

The image of fruit being produced raises another issue inherent in Isaiah 40:24. When the world's rulers and lawmakers are brought to naught, their works are revealed for their true value. This image, too, is reinforced in the New Testament when the apostle Paul writes about our works being tested by fire so that what we are and what we have done with our lives are manifested (1 Corinthians 3:12-13). When tested by the LORD's blowing or fire, our works wither and are carried away if they are merely impermanent works of stubble.

Do we live in the light of eternity? Are we spending our time and abilities to do what withers, things that are mere straw and will be blown away, things that indicate our own lack of rooting? Or are we grounded in the faith of the community and in the community of faith so that what we do has permanent value, so that when our work is tested by fire it will be revealed as truly eternal?

Many pastors tell me that they don't have time to read — to which I want to respond that we don't have eternity not to. In a Web site commentary on my book about worship, Craig Loscalzo reported that a mentor once told him that "preachers should always be in the process of reading a book of the Bible, a novel, a work of classical theology, and a current piece of theological wisdom at all times." That sounds impossible, but I am grateful for that observation. If I am to do work that lasts, my teaching needs to be rooted in God's Word for sure — and then also in the needs of the times (communicated to me by novels and in-depth news magazines) and the historic understandings of the Church throughout the ages (learned from a balance of classical and contemporary theology).

Our culture is dying because of its lack of depth. Those of us who serve the world by being servants of the Church can offer great gifts to our neighbors if we ourselves are rooted enough to pass on the eternal truths of the faith, with the nontransitory authority of Christ himself.

To what does Paul refer when he writes of "works of gold" in 1 Corinthians 3? Every time I stop to reflect on what really matters out of whatever I do, I am overwhelmed with the realization that the only things that really count are those that contribute to others' knowing Christ and being set free by his grace and love. If all of us are only grass, our time is best spent proclaiming what stands forever and rooting people deeply in that Word. Is my life invested in those top priorities? Is yours?

These questions are appropriate not only for professional church workers and the "princes" of the world. One of the major failures of many contemporary churches is that we are not "[equipping] the saints for the work of ministry" (Ephesians 4:12). Christians might have many occupations, but the *vocation* of all of us is to be agents of the Kingdom of God — offering to all our neighbors the good news of God's mercy in Jesus Christ, of God's forgiveness and healing and direction, of moral truth and living hope. Let us pray that we will be open to the possibilities God presents us to bring his love and grace to our needy world by being actively engaged in feeding the hungry, sheltering the homeless, caring for the ill and for those in prison. In an increasingly calloused and violent world, may we who are God's people be speakers of truth, builders of justice and peace, and searchers for national and international policies that really address the profound issues that are tearing our country and world apart. May the Church and all its members be a beacon of light and trust, a community of caring and God's salvation.

QUESTIONS FOR FURTHER MEDITATION:

1. *In what vain things have I mistakenly planted myself?*
2. *What will help me become more securely rooted in Christ?*

3. What works have I done that seemed strong and lasting and good, but turned out to be or were shown to be merely stubble?

4. What kinds of things dry me up? What sorts of whirlwinds blow me away?

5. What will make the difference between difficulties drying me up and the same trials causing me to dig my roots down more deeply to get the moisture I need?

6. What could my congregation be doing to help its members get rooted more thoroughly?

7. How could I help my congregation to understand itself better as a community that passes on a faith already rooted and established?

25 *The Cry of God's Holiness*

> *"To whom then will you compare me,*
> *that I should be equal?" says the Holy One.*
>
> Isaiah 40:25 (composite)

Consider Bjorn Borg. When I first wrote this book, he had just won his third straight Wimbledon tennis championship. This was the first time someone had done that for more than forty years. Suppose he said to us, "Now, to whom will you compare me, that I could be as good as he?" Or what if we asked the same question about the returned-from-retirement Michael Jordan, who, as I rewrite this, has just led the Chicago Bulls to a new record of NBA wins and to the NBA championship — again!

"Borg and Jordan *as good as* someone else?" we would exclaim. What an absurd question. They are better than anyone else in all the world!

That is the irony of *YHWH*'s question in verse 25. "To whom will you liken me," the Holy One says, "to be comparable?" Of course, *YHWH* is unparalleled, unrivaled, unequaled. What or who could be set up as similar in value to the LORD? According

149

to Hebrew law, if I killed your ox, I would have to give you a sum of money equivalent to its worth. Similarly, the Holy One asks, "What could you put up, that I should match the funds?"

The question is so backward that it is ludicrous. The LORD is infinitely more than a mere countervailing equal. Indeed, God does not just equal, but is incalculably beyond everything and everyone put all together all at once.

For the first time in this fortieth chapter, *YHWH* calls himself the Holy One, a name frequently used elsewhere in the book of Isaiah. The Hebrew term, *kadosh,* means that God is separated, set apart in his purity. Vessels that were *kadosh* were isolated for use in the temple because they had been particularly consecrated by the Israelite priests. *YHWH,* on the other hand, is separated because holiness is his very character. No one or nothing can be compared to *YHWH,* for none else is so matchlessly alone.

The irony of the question that God asks heightens the uniqueness of his characterization as the "Holy One." Immediately there comes to my mind the man with an unclean spirit who, upon meeting Jesus, cried out, "What have you to do with us, Jesus of Nazareth? . . . I know who you are, the Holy One of God" (Mark 1:24). His shuddering terror underscores evil's incapacity before purity. The unclean spirit could not stand before the holiness of Jesus; the Holy One cast him out.

Evil cannot tolerate a vision of holiness, nor can the Holy One tolerate the presence of evil. Consequently, the name *Holy One,* as applied to God, must fill us with genuine fear (offset, of course, by the dialectical recognition of God's sanctifying — that is, holiness-producing — grace). This is the atmosphere in the narrative of the calling of Isaiah in chapter 6. Isaiah sees the Holy One, high and lifted up, with his train filling the temple. The cherubim and seraphim sing antiphonally, crying out, "Holy, holy, holy is the LORD of hosts; the whole earth is full of his glory" (6:3). Immediately

Isaiah reacts with fear. Overwhelmed with guilt and grief, he cries out, "Woe is me! I am lost, for I am a man of unclean lips . . . yet my eyes have seen the King, the LORD of hosts!" (6:5). When we are confronted with the holiness of God, we cannot help but acknowledge the total absence of holiness in our lives, our complete lack of worth in the presence of *YHWH*.

I grew up understanding this proper fear because my parents taught me to know awe in our worship services. I was astounded, then, when recently I couldn't persuade some young adults whom I was training that certain rowdy campfire-type songs are quite blasphemous if used for worship. Worship services in many churches have become so casual — even flippant — so much focused on the immanence of God that children have no comprehension of the infinite chasm between us and the transcendently HOLY God.

We experience glimpses of this jarring contrast sometimes in mere human terms. For example, consider how you would feel if Michael Jordan or someone incredibly brilliant, enormously wealthy, or stunningly beautiful sat beside you. You could hardly help but compare yourself and realize your inferiority. I always felt so small as a beginning organ student in college when some of the real musicians, who had been playing for years, would hear us perform our first-year recital pieces. When we multiply that embarrassment a relentless number of times and then add a load of guilt and shame besides, we can begin to discover what it is like to face the holiness of God.

Critical to the background of the Reformation was Martin Luther's unique terror and trepidation because he did not know how to please the Holy One. He tried everything — doing every conceivable sort of penance, beating his own body mercilessly, confessing the smallest of sins and even some he had not committed — and yet he was utterly aware that he could never please a holy God.

When we put that sense of *YHWH's* holiness into the context of this verse, we are aghast at human audacity. What presumption that we should think we could compare anything to God! What arrogance to think that we can worship God glibly, turning him into a buddy, with no sense of the infinite distance between us mere creatures and our sovereign Creator — not to mention the chasm dredged by our sinfulness.

Any time people confronted the holiness of the LORD in the Bible — even when it was glimpsed through the appearance of his angels — they reacted with fear, even falling on their faces. How can we recover that deep awareness of God's infinite separateness in our irreverent culture, without losing the dialectical balance of God's equally infinite compassion for us broken people? I am not asking for terror. Genuine, healthy fear of God is counterbalanced with an equally deep sense of God's gracious love — but we don't understand that mercy well if we make grace cheap by neglecting God's holiness.

Other attributes of God are intertwined with his holiness. *YHWH's* perfect holiness also, of necessity, embodies perfect Truth. We can confidently trust that our relationship with God is the ultimate reality. We can believe that God will be totally faithful to his character. We can be confident that he will always be the same yesterday, today, and forever in eternity (Hebrews 13:8). His holiness implies consistency; the holiness of God's love means constancy.

For that reason, as Luther discovered (and found himself set free by it), we can come boldly into the presence of the Holy One. We know that the constancy of his grace and the perfection of his love are fully incarnated in his Son, who came to secure holiness for us. Why don't churches teach more thoroughly that Christ has already made us saints?

What Joy can fill our Christian lives because God has set us apart already by grace. When Leviticus 20:26 (see also 1 Peter

1:16) records *YHWH* saying, "You shall be holy to me; for I the LORD am holy, and have separated you from the peoples, that you should be mine" (RSV), that should not be interpreted to mean that we'd better shape up and become holy as God is. No, the words are rather a promise that we shall indeed be holy. We do not become holy by extended effort, but because the Holy One has already made us so. When in the narrative of chapter 6 Isaiah confessed his unholiness, an angel flew to him with tongs holding a burning coal. Cleansing was completed, and Isaiah was sent out to be the messenger of the LORD. His grief over his uncleanness was transformed into eagerness to serve.

The process is the same for us. The First Letter of John emphasizes that "if we confess our sins, he who is faithful and just will forgive us our sins and cleanse us from all unrighteousness" (1:9). That the LORD provided for our cleansing is part of his character as the Holy One. In his holiness, he desires fellowship with a holy people. He has planned for his people to be set apart, separated from the world, in order to offer it an alternative.

How can we compare the LORD to anything else? We must ask that question again in light of God's holiness. When we realize afresh that *YHWH* alone is holy, it is a shattering discovery. We couldn't survive it if we didn't also know the perfection of his grace and the fullness of our holy calling.

QUESTIONS FOR FURTHER MEDITATION:

1. How is the holiness of God revealed?

2. How might I define the word "holy"?

3. How does the holiness of God present to me both the law and the gospel?

4. What does my congregation do or what could it do to convey the holiness of God in our worship?

5. *What does it mean for my daily life that God sees me as holy through Christ?*

6. *How can I avoid the extremes of thinking I can create my own holiness and despairing because I can't?*

7. *How will my holiness reveal itself?*

26 *The Cry of Personal Significance*

Lift up your eyes on high
and see who has created these [stars].
The One who leads forth their host by number
He calls them all by name;
Because of the greatness of His might
and the strength of His power
not one [of them] is missing.

Isaiah 40:26 (NAS)

Gazing at the incredible display of stars, I lay awake half the night. All the women from our choir and all the female students of the Christian Medical College in Vellore, India, were sleeping out on the roof of the dorm. It hadn't rained for years, and the sky was "crystal clear." (I don't think I ever really knew the meaning of that phrase until that night.) I had never known there were so many stars and was awestruck by the grandeur of God visible in their splendor. Each time I closed my eyes, I had to open them right up again to make sure that all that radiance was still there.

We can't be certain that verse 26 is speaking about the stars, because the word for them does not occur in the original Hebrew, but the prophet's comments seem to suggest them. "Lift up on high your eyes and see," he commands. The first verb is an imperative form of the one we discussed in verses 4, 11, and 24 in connection with the lifting of the valleys, the lambs, and the world's rulers. Now the listeners are urged to lift up their own eyes in order to observe more carefully. When they have done so, they will be forced by what they have seen to ask, "Who created these?" The standard demonstrative pronoun translated "these" could refer to anything observable on high, but stars seem to be the most likely object.

The description of the Creator of these heavenly objects begins with a participial construction that says literally, "The bringer-out by number of their host." Unless otherwise specified (as in the phrase "the hosts of Israel"), this last term is associated with the heavenly hosts, as in the most common expression, "The LORD of hosts." All the armies of angels, all the beings of the heavens, are suggested.

The One bringing them out does so by number. The singular form of this term suggests individuality. He brings them out personally, one by one, as if to count them off.

That individual attention is accentuated by the next phrase, "to all of them by name he calls." The same personal care is manifest in the image of Jesus as the Good Shepherd. Jesus asserts in John 10:3 that the Good Shepherd knows his sheep, calls them by name, and leads them out. In Isaiah 40 the Creator, who was also called a Shepherd in verse 11, is pictured with the same specificity, calling out all the hosts of heaven individually, by name. The imperfect — uncompleted action — form of the verb suggests not the original naming of those beings, but a continual calling. The picture can be humorously graphic. Each night God summons, "Okay, Polaris, you can come out now. All right, Betelgeuse, it's your turn."

156

Furthermore, because of the "great might and powerful strength" of the "Bringer," not one is missing. The four terms used to describe God's omnipotence will be more significant when we study verse 29, where they are used again and reveal a progression in thought. At this point only the first of the four is a term of quantity, meaning "much." The other three terms suggest almightiness.

Because of their Bringer's power, not one of the host is missing. The Hebrew sentence actually says, "A man [*ish*] is not missing." Such anthropomorphism accentuates the verse's individualizing. Since the text also includes the term *hosts,* which suggests military forces, my first Hebrew professor quipped, "Not even a private is out of the ranks." The picture is a graphic image of the "great might and powerful strength" of *YHWH.* Not one of all the myriads upon myriads of stars will ever fall without his knowing. He is able both to call each one forth by name and to hold each one in its perfectly appointed place.

Verse 26 is stupendously comforting. The dazzling display of the starry hosts reminds us that God is so transcendent that he controls the galaxies and so immanent that he knows each star by name.

The stars have always turned human thought to what is larger than ourselves — so that many cultures tried to chart the future by them. The stars and planets enabled the Magi to find the Messiah. The night our mission tour choir sang a concert in Bethlehem at the Evangelical Lutheran Christmas Church (now a vital center for defending the rights of native Palestinians), the sky was ablaze with stars. Although it was July 19, their brilliance and loveliness lifted our thoughts irresistibly to the Nativity — and we sang carols on the bus all the way back to Jerusalem.

Lift up your eyes on high and see: Who created these? Does not the beauty of the heavens elevate you beyond your self and your idolatries? Our modern telescopes, spaceships, and the

Hubble telescope search galaxies beyond galaxies, and yet they cannot comprehend the infinity of stardom.

Furthermore, God calls each one of the host by name. They aren't just a vast array of meaningless bright fires or reflections, but they have a distinctive character, a quality all their own. If God is really GOD, after all, then he has called out each dimension of his creation personally. God is behind every process, every development, every change, every birth — and gives to each creation or body its nature, its function, its characteristics, its uniqueness.

How very specific God has been in creating each of us. Ponder the multitudes of planets and stars and then think about the billions of people inhabiting the earth — yet each one is distinct. You and I are each unique in name in the biblical sense, which means our character. God calls us forth uniquely and cares for us personally. In Isaiah 43:1, the LORD says, "I have called you by name, you are mine."

Finally, Isaiah 40:26 reminds us that God's plan is so perfect and his omnipotence so complete that never is anything missing. Jesus says, "Consider the lilies . . . and the birds of the air" (Matthew 6:25-34). Here we realize that even all the falling stars are counted. Even the very hairs of our heads are numbered.

Do we really believe that? (The next verse will indict us because we don't.) How much more freely we would live if we trusted God's personal care for stars and lilies and birds. Jesus asks, "How much more deeply" does God care for us? Never is anyone missing — by the LORD's pure grace and great power.

Mother Teresa and her Sisters of Charity model for us God's particular care through their ministrations to each dying person they encounter. How can we, too, be more involved in God's tender attention for each one around us?

QUESTIONS FOR FURTHER MEDITATION:

1. *What besides the stars in their vast array lifts me beyond myself to look for the God behind it all?*

2. *How is the contrast of the vast array and yet God's individual attention to each member of the vast array revealed to me?*

3. *When and how did God call me by name? How did I become aware of God's call?*

4. *How do I know that each one of us is important to God?*

5. *What can my congregation do to help each person know that he or she is important to the Christian community and to God?*

6. *What am I doing to bring God's personal care to those forgotten by the world?*

7. *What is my congregational community doing to be God's personal care for the forgotten of our neighborhood? Of the world?*

27 *The Cry against Complaining*

Why do you say, O Jacob, and speak, O Israel,
  "My way is hidden from the LORD,
  and my right is disregarded by my God"?

Isaiah 40:27

Mother caught us swiping cookies. My brother and I thought we could get away without her seeing us. Sometimes it seemed that she had eyes in the back of her head. Our way could not be hidden from her.

Isaiah 40:27 criticizes the Israelites collectively for thinking that their way was hidden from *YHWH*. The Hebrew word translated "way" in the New Revised Standard Version means one's life undertakings or daily conduct. The verb is in a perfect form, which implies a completed action — that Israel's patterns of behavior are already hidden. Together these word choices suggest that the Hebrew people think their trend of life can escape or has escaped God's notice.

The poetic parallel says literally, "and from *Elohim* my judgment is passed over." The same word for judgment occurred previously in verse 14 and might imply either a negative sentence or a positive justice. The verb "to pass over" is the one used to speak of fording a river to get beyond it. It might suggest that the sentence Jacob should be under is not being executed.

Together these two lines could be interpreted either in the sense of Jacobean deceptiveness (the meaning of that name and the actions of that patriarch) or in the sense of the typical Israelite complaining. In the first sense, the descendants of Jacob would be exulting, "God doesn't see our misbehavior. We don't have to worry because we can escape the sentence we deserve." In the second sense, they would be mourning, "God just doesn't see our lot; our rights are being disregarded by our God."

Both interpretations fit in with the prophet's pointed question, "Why do you say [this], O Jacob, and speak [in this way], O Israel?" Both cunning and complaint contradict the attitudes of people who know and love their God. Both interpretations offer us significant lessons concerning our attitudes about God's relationship with us and his action in our lives.

First of all, the prophet's admonitions are certainly necessary. Why did the Israelites react as they did? Why do we? What gives us cause to complain or to seek to deceive God and get away with apathy or disobedience? Isaiah 40 reminds God's people throughout history that it is impossible for our way to be hidden from YHWH, much as we might like to try. Our road certainly can't be hidden from the One who doesn't allow even one of the stars to be missing. On the basis of the evidence in the last verse, why would we say, like Jacob, that God doesn't observe our behavior? Why would we think, like Israel, that our rights are being disregarded by our God? Surely we need the rhetorical questions of the next verse to remind us that we ought to pay better attention to what we have known and heard.

It is impossible to hide from the LORD, and yet how often we think we do. We think we can escape his sentence and the judgment we deserve. We think we can get into the cookies without being noticed.

But our sin will find us out. We can't get away from the consequences of our deceptions. When we lie, we have to tell other lies to cover up the first. When we trick others, we lose their trust and spoil our relationships. When we act contrary to our Christian principles, our consciences plague us and perhaps cause us to suffer physically. Ultimately, sin always produces its own destructive consequences from which we can't escape. We choose our own judgment.

On the other hand, the second possibility for interpretation of this text confronts us with our blind folly at those times when we judge God. We shout that he doesn't act toward us as we deserve, that life isn't fair. We demand justice and cry to secure our rights.

In contrast, the apostle Paul offers us the model of Christ Jesus, who, though he was God, did not demand his rights as God (Philippians 2:5-11). He genuinely deserved them, but he didn't demand them. We don't deserve them, but we insist that we get them. When we honestly consider our character as the self-centered people we are (apart from the grace of God), we must be appalled at the presumption of our complaints. Our gripes about the particulars of our lives surmise that YHWH doesn't know our troubles, that he doesn't care if we suffer injustice, that he isn't being fair.

We can't change these foolish feelings merely by telling ourselves that we are wrong. We need instead to learn to know God better in order to trust more thoroughly his purposes in our lives.

First, let us celebrate that God does not deal with us fairly, for, though we don't deserve it, he gives us the right of being his children (John 1:12). On the basis of God's gift of the "rights" to salvation (in the largest sense of that word) and eternal life (already begun), we can gladly give up other rights for the sake of the Kingdom of God. Jesus calls us "blessed" when we do so (Matthew 5:3-11).

U.S. culture is being torn apart by more and more victim groups clamoring for their "rights." Those who love God will certainly work for genuine justice for those whose true rights have been denied them; but there are occasions when we might (and should) forego our own rights for the sake of others. Certainly God cares about our rights, but he also calls us to pass on his care for others. If he never lets a star fall without his attention, certainly it matters to him what happens to us. On the basis of the picture of God in verse 26, the prophet asks the question of this verse, in anticipation of the rebuke in verse 28.

The indictment in this verse is indispensable for our culture of complaint. We can so easily get caught up in this bitter and grumbling spirit that we don't realize what our murmuring and discontent say about the LORD. To whine is to accuse him of not being aware of what is going on. To snivel about our situation suggests that we think our way is hidden from his wise purposes.

Someone sent me a card long ago that read, "The Lord gives the best to those who leave the choice with him." I often forget that, insist on my own way, believe that my sense of justice is better than God's. What foolish idolatry to place our own intelligence above the LORD's wisdom. And how much of God's best we must miss by demanding our own inferior preferences. Our constant lack of trust violates the first commandment, makes it impossible for us to love the LORD our God with our whole heart and soul and *mind*.

In the Christian community we can learn from those with a sure and mature faith, who know that God fully perceives our way, that all things do indeed work together for good to them that love God (Romans 8:28). That frequently misinterpreted

163

verse does not say that all things *are* good, but only that eventually God works them around to produce good — if our love for him makes us receptive to receiving that benefit.

Isaiah 40:27 makes me ashamed. So often I act as if my way were hidden from God — as if he doesn't care about all the hardships in my life because of handicaps, or as if he didn't care about justice. So often I am guilty of thinking that I know better than God what is appropriate and right. When I lost my vision for seven months because of retinal hemorrhaging in my good eye, I was so busy complaining and fearing that I missed out on the blessedness of fellowship with God I could have experienced if I had trusted that God knew my way and would bring good out of it.

I am thankful that God doesn't deal with me according to my deceptions and complaints.

QUESTIONS FOR FURTHER MEDITATION:

1. *How have I experienced the truth that I can't get away with sin?*

2. *What were some incidents in the history of Israel in which the people thought their sin was hidden from God?*

3. *How can I avoid a complaining and contentious spirit?*

4. *Does the fact that Christians many times have to suffer injustice contradict this verse?*

5. *Which campaigns for rights should Christians join?*

6. *How can I learn to give up my rights voluntarily?*

7. *How could my congregation be involved in securing the rights of others in our local community?*

28 *The Cry of* YHWH's *Everlastingness*

Have you not known? Have you not heard?
The LORD is the everlasting God,
    the Creator of the ends of the earth.
He does not faint or grow weary;
    his understanding is unsearchable.

Isaiah 40:28

Have you ever talked with a child first exploring the idea of infinity?

"You mean there is no beginning and no end?"
Right.
"It just goes on and on and on and never stops?"
Uh huh. Like a circle except never the same as it goes on and on.
"But it's got to start somewhere!"
Huh uh.
"How can it be like that?"
Who knows?

165

Can anyone explain how God is eternal or imagine the impossible prospect and incredible possibility of our own everlasting existence in God's presence?

Infinity is the theme of this verse. Its tones ring out not only in the words and phrases themselves but also in the Hebrew constructions and the progression of thought from previous verses.

The verse begins with the same admonishment as the opening of verse 21, but with two noteworthy changes. First, in verse 21, the phrases "Do you not know? Are you not hearing?" utilize a second person plural verb, whereas here the form is singular in keeping with verse 27, in which the people were addressed collectively, as one — as Jacob and Israel.

Second, the verb construction has changed from an imperfect form, which signifies uncompleted action, to a perfect form, which indicates a completed action. In verse 21 the people are literally asked, "Are you still not knowing?" and "will you not hear?" Here the questions have become, "Have you not known? Have you not heard?" After the prophet's criticism of their complaining, he seems almost to be saying, "This is your last chance, Israel. You ought to have understood by now." Thus he ushers in the final argument of the chapter, which will be developed in four verses dancing around the theme of not becoming faint or growing weary.

Immediately after the indicting questions, *YHWH* is defined by his relationship to timelessness. The Hebrew form of the words actually means that the only "God of everlastingness" is *YHWH,* the covenant "I AM" of the Hebrew people. Then three pictures follow which enable us to observe how his everlastingness can be recognized.

First, *YHWH* is the "Creator of the ends of the earth." Not only did this God create all the earth and everything in it, but he also set its boundaries. For the Israelites this meant that God created beyond what they knew. Now, when we know an enormous amount more about the farthest parts of the cosmos, we still cannot fathom its limits, but we know that God is beyond those boundaries as their beginning and end.

Second, "Not does he become faint or grow weary." As is obvious, and as later verses will emphasize, others do become tired. Here the verb is in an imperfect form of continuous action to underscore that God perpetually does not become faint or weak.

Finally, "Not is there to be searching of his understanding." The preposition introducing his sagacity means "as far as" or "penetration of," and the noun for "understanding" is the same one we met at the end of verse 14. (The same root had also occurred in a verb form at the beginning of that verse.) No searching can penetrate his comprehension. Both of these last two phrases begin with *not* in the Hebrew. Never will God grow tired; never will he be understood. *YHWH* grasps everything; we can only barely begin to imagine him because his love encompasses us.

The prophet's rhetorical questions respond to the previous complaints by the people about God's lack of justice. The progression of verses emphasizes that if the people would have known and heard (as suggested previously) they wouldn't be inveigling or griping as they were. The critical element is what they should have known — namely, the everlastingness of their covenant God. God's purposes from before all of time extend into time and go right on through time on our behalf. Because the I AM is boundless, we can trust his plans to unfold without limits.

Everlastingness in God's creation means that all things are under his control. By his great might and powerful strength (verse 26), nothing is missing, nothing escapes the LORD's notice. Surely our way cannot be hidden from the One who sees to the ends of the earth.

Furthermore, the LORD does not become faint or grow

167

weary. Not only did he create the world, but he continues to preserve it. Not only did he save us, but he continues to work in us to transform us into his likeness and to fulfill his purposes through us. Not only does the LORD establish us, but he continues to care and to provide for us and to sustain us.

Isn't it hard to imagine that God is never tired? In our stress and busyness, we can't begin to fathom not needing naps. We can't help but chuckle at how this anthropomorphic picture forces us to stop and acknowledge that this is GOD, after all, about whom we are talking.

It would buoy us immensely if more often in our burdens of busyness we would pause to imagine how God works constantly, watching over everything, all at once, all the time — and yet he's not tired tomorrow. Nor does he go to sleep tonight. We can call on him in the middle of the night. We can call on him time and time and time again, and all of us can call on him at once, and he remains patient and forbearing, ready to receive and answer our cries. He never grows weary of helping the oppressed, the needy, the comfortless, the desolate.

The process theologians who make God less than able, not almighty, need the next phrase from the prophet that *YHWH's* "understanding is unsearchable." Even though we cannot figure out why God behaves toward us as he does, we cannot attribute it to his being tired or powerless to help. Rather, we must recognize that we cannot penetrate God's infinite wisdom. This gives an especially specific response to the previous verse and enables us to have hope in our waiting. When God does not intervene as we wish, when things don't change as we hope, it is not because God is not able or does not will it. He has reasons infinitely beyond our understanding; many mysteries of God are not yet unfolded.

That the LORD's understanding is unsearchable gives a foundation for much of the rest of Isaiah 40. We don't comprehend why the grass is blown away. We can't unravel the problem of pain. But God knows, and we can trust that his character is to be just and gracious and righteous. We believe that his understanding is right, truly in accordance with genuine reality, even though we cannot decipher it. Consequently, we are driven to a deeper love for his infinite care. Without growing weary of us, the LORD is everlastingly devoted to us.

I grow very weary in devotion. I can't imagine that God never gets tired of me. My needs seem so important to me, but, scrutinized against an eternal perspective, they're not so significant. Yet we allow ourselves to be dominated by our worries and controlled by our anxieties. Why do I worry about God's provision when I should have known that he does not grow weary of caring? Haven't I heard that he knows my needs and understands (better than I do) what I am going through?

One of the most precious assurances for our humanity, certainly, is that Jesus has undergone every temptation and trial to which we are subject, so that he eternally understands (Hebrews 4:15). Who can begin to comprehend how deeply he discerns — since he knows our feelings both from a human perspective and from God's everlasting wisdom!

When I first wrote this book almost twenty years ago, I was experiencing the deepest depression of my life. I had been deceived and my life had been torn apart by two very close friends, and I couldn't put the pieces of my self back together. One night, engulfed in a black gloom, I screamed at God, "You don't understand. You don't know what it's like to be so bitterly betrayed!" O Jesus! At last I might be beginning to recognize the suffering you bore for me!

Verse 28 makes me want to cry out with Job, "Though he slay me, yet will I trust in him" (13:15, KJV), or with Habakkuk,

Though the fig tree does not blossom,
  and no fruit is on the vines; . . .

yet I will rejoice in the LORD;
    I will exult in the God of my salvation.
GOD, the Lord, is my strength;
    he makes my feet like the feet of a deer,
    and makes me tread upon the heights. (3:17-19)

God's understanding is unsearchable, but we believe that it in-cludes trustworthy purposes for us. God is unweary in faithfulness and well-doing.

It's time for you and me to know. Pay attention now, and let us hear. For *YHWH* is the God of everlasting good.

QUESTIONS FOR FURTHER MEDITATION:

1. What kinds of things help me to know and to hear better as I continue growing in my Christian life?

2. How can I describe God's everlastingness?

3. How does the fact of God's everlastingness affect my rela-tionship with him in daily life?

4. How does my behavior (unconsciously?) indicate that I think God is powerless or has limited understanding in some situations?

5. Do my prayers sometimes sound as if I'm saying, "God, if you knew all the facts, I'm sure you'd do it my way"?

6. How does it comfort me to know that God's understanding is unsearchable?

7. How would greater consciousness of God's everlastingness change my Christian community?

29 *The Cry of Empowering*

He gives power to the faint,
and strengthens the powerless.

Isaiah 40:29

Clifford Schultz, one of the mightiest men I have ever known, was almost completely incapacitated by advancing multiple sclerosis. The vibrancy of his faith and witness and the depth of his love and compassion moved literally hundreds of people. He always had a good word of encouragement for everyone he met, especially the other patients at the convalescent home where he lived. All who visited him were uplifted by his strength. No one could ever doubt who was the Source and Giver of Clifford's immense resilience.

The prophet does a fascinating thing with word choices in this verse to accentuate the strength of that Giver. He makes use of several words from verses 26 and 28 to underscore the relationship and the contrast between God and human beings. The contrast is further heightened by a change in the proportion of terms of quantity and of power from verse 26. A careful look

171

at all these special word choices multiplies the impact of this verse on our lives.

The Hebrew of verse 29 begins with a participial phrase; that *YHWH* is the subject is understood. The prophet calls him "The One giving to the faint strength." The word for "faint" is the first of the two qualities denied in the character of God in verse 28, and the word for "strength" is the final term of the four ascribed to God in verse 26. Thus, to those not like him in their weakness, the LORD imparts a bit of himself. He confers upon them his strength.

The poetic parallel, "and to the one without might he increases vastness," uses two other terms from verse 26. The word for "might" is the second of the four words that make up the series describing God's omnipotence. There God possesses it; here human beings are without it. The verb translated "increases" in this verse is the root verb form of the first term in the verse 26 series. The only term that is not repeated in verse 29 from that series is the third word, which we translated "powerful." In its place is substituted a Hebrew word that sounds very much like it, so perhaps the poet/prophet intended a play on words. This new term, instead of stressing the idea of power, signifies vastness or multiplication or making more tangible. In other words, on behalf of the one lacking might *YHWH* increases the multiplication of it.

The Hebrew thought pattern that underlies this image ties in with the Hebrew emphasis on numbers. When the First Testament people used such multiplied terms, they didn't think of them as just being added together, but as multiplied to the second term's power. For example, the phrase "ages upon ages" does not simply mean ages plus ages, but it signifies ages times ages times ages to the "agesth" power. A similar thought pattern underlies our expression "multiplied to the 'nth' degree." Here, then, the prophet proclaims that God increases might to a limitless degree.

This striking image is reinforced by the progression from verse 26, which can now be specified. There God was described with three terms of power and only one term of quantity. Here in verse 29, what he does for human beings is asserted with two terms of power and a deliberate increase (emphasized by a play on words) to two terms of quantity. God possesses such enormous power that when he gives it to human beings, theirs must be multiplied to a double degree.

We all experience times when we have no strength left. What a comfort it is at such times that our God of "great might and powerful strength," who never gets tired himself, passes on his fortitude to his people. He gives vigor to us when we are exhausted. In fact, his power flows through us best when we are powerless.

Church history astounds us with the mighty things God has drawn out of the weakness of his people. The Church in general and specific saints in particular — humble people like Francis of Assisi or William Carey — have manifested extraordinary strength in the face of seemingly insurmountable obstacles. I'm especially eager, however, for us to recognize how this verse is true, not only for the contemporary churches in general, but for ourselves in particular, by God's grace.

That was demonstrated so clearly by my friend Clifford. He had a tremendously eternal mind enclosed in a terribly confining body, limited to little physical movement. His constant struggle against pain and limitation finally ended when he died of cancer. Clifford deeply understood other people, and his faith and zeal for evangelism were a constant inspiration for me. He knew so well how to draw his strength from the LORD.

I remember one day when, while pushing his wheelchair through the halls on our way to sing for other patients, I was thinking about what an exertion life was for him. He strained to breathe. He could barely hold on to my guitar lying on the table of his wheelchair, and he travailed laboriously to speak and sing (though he still told everyone he met about the great love of his Savior Jesus Christ). As I was pondering his afflictions, he suddenly exclaimed to me, "You know, Marva, life is so wonderful down here it's hard to imagine that heaven will be even better. But it will be!" I was so ashamed. Clifford patiently endured all his sufferings, and he never gave up or grumbled. He never uttered the complaints of Isaiah 40:27, as I so often do. He knew so well the promise of strength in verse 29, and his love for the LORD overpowered everything else. His heart, mind, and spirit were so eternally fixed that the limitations of his body were surmounted with great struggle and greater Joy.

Clifford always had more than enough strength to carry on his ministry, even in the weakest of times. To a lesser degree, I have understood this verse most clearly at times when I have felt inadequate and incapable. At those times, I am amazed at how God accomplishes his purposes through us — in spite of us. What is stunning about verse 29 is the realization that we never do really begin to discover the power of God until we learn our own weaknesses.

Although I don't have the space here to discuss in detail the theology of weakness inherent in the following comments,[1] the message of God's strength in 2 Corinthians 12:9 is uncommon. After Paul besought the Lord three times to remove his "thorn in the flesh," the Lord answered him, "My grace is sufficient for you, for your power is *brought to its finish* in weakness" (my translation). There is no pronoun (*your* or *my*) in the Greek original before the word *power,* and the verb that is usually translated "made perfect" in this verse is the same verb that Jesus cried from the cross when

1. See Marva J. Dawn, *Joy in Our Weakness,* a study of the book of Revelation and a theology of suffering (St. Louis: Concordia Publishing House, 1994).

his work was ended. Every time that verb appears in the New Testament, it is translated "to bring to the finish," with the one exception of 2 Corinthians 12:9. If we brought the customary meaning of that verb to bear on that verse also, we would know more clearly how God's strength is available to us.

When we are weak, we no longer try to exert our useless power. It is brought to its end, and we become yielded vessels. Then God can really begin to exert his power *through us* to reach out to others. That is what Clifford demonstrated so profoundly. Having no strength of his own, he was an almost perfectly pliable tool in God's hands. With his power ended, God's power could come through Clifford more strongly than almost anyone else I've ever known. "I will glory in my weaknesses then," the apostle Paul concludes literally, "that the power of God may tabernacle upon me." Oh, to have that kind of attitude!

Do we take God up on his promise? Are we able to receive his strength? We can never know God's power unless we attempt the impossible. As long as we are doing things that are within our capabilities, things for which we are qualified and skilled, we can too easily trust our own gifts (forgetting that those come from God also). Only when we try to do things beyond us will we end our attempts at power, dependently turn to the LORD, and rely solely on him.

One of the reasons why we need the Christian community is to help us discover this truth together, to learn to receive the power of God that is available to us. Let us grasp the visions from *YHWH* that allow us to move out boldly in his name (that is, his character) and by his strength. Too often churches wait around until they gather all the kinds of resources they think they'll need to undertake certain tasks. By the time they begin the tasks, however, it is too often too late, and the crisis needing ministry is past or changed.

Individuals and churches could proceed so much more boldly with missions that they know to be the LORD's will. We can trust that God will multiply doubly the strengths we need to accomplish his purposes. Most of the churches that are truly growing today (that is, deeper, and not just fatter) are those that pursue issues boldly, creating ministries to match the needs they see, and trusting that God will provide the strength of finances and personnel.

The key to it all lies in knowing the One who is the Giver and Multiplier of strength. We might be faint or lack the necessary might, but that is irrelevant. In fact, it is better that way, because then our power can be brought to its end and instead God's power can be multiplied through us on behalf of others. We are just "earthen vessels," Paul says in 2 Corinthians 4:7 (RSV), but in our old clay pots we hold an unspeakable treasure. The fact that we are weak is of great benefit. Then everyone can see that the transcendent power definitely belongs to God and not to us.

QUESTIONS FOR FURTHER MEDITATION:

1. What forms does the strength of God take when he gives it to me?

2. What have been some particular times when I have been weary and have experienced God's gift of strength?

3. What kinds of things make me weak or destroy my might?

4. How can I use those things to be channels for God's strength rather than sources of bitterness and complaint?

5. Do I have to be weak or attempt impossible things to know the power of God?

6. What persons whom I know manifest the way the LORD gives strength to the faint?

7. In what directions might my church undertake new ministries more boldly, trusting God to provide the necessary resources and strength?

30 *The Cry of Human Limitation*

Even youths will faint and be weary,
and the young will fall exhausted.

Isaiah 40:30

How could the little boy have so much energy? The son of one of my best friends, he was about four years old at the time. He could run around nonstop, falling, picking himself up again, and charging on into life from early in the morning until late at night. His mother couldn't keep up with him. Where did he get all that vitality? Yet even he collapsed into bed at night and slept soundly. From the way he expended energy during the day, one might almost begin to think he would never be tired.

That is the picture verse 30 uses to compare human beings to *YHWH*. "Even lads become faint and grow weary," the prophet observes. Both of these terms describing human weakness and fatigue are identical to the ones asserted in verse 27 to be absent from the character of the LORD. How opposite we are — even those of whom we would least expect it, those who seem at first glance to have limitless energy.

177

The second line of the couplet is a marvelous example of poetic intensification. Both the subject and the verb from the first line are magnified in these words: "and young men shall fall exhausted." Now the line speaks actually of the firstborn, not to call attention to that fact itself, but to stress its implications: The firstborn are the ones chosen for a double portion, the ones to carry on the family name. In other words, now we are speaking of the cream of the crop. The verb is made more acute by its form; the infinitive absolute actually means "stumbling, they shall stumble." It is the form used in Genesis to indicate the absolute surety of death — "dying, they shall die" — and means here the certainty, the incontrovertibility of the stumbling of those in their prime.

Together these two lines declare, "Even those of whom we wouldn't expect it will become faint and grow weary [which never happens to the God of everlastingness], and the very best of those, the most vigorous, will surely stumble badly." No one can miss the prophet's insistence on the total feebleness of human beings. We think we can get by on our own strength, at least when we're younger, but this verse reminds us that everyone is subject to the same malady.

This verse catches me, because I'm especially prone to stumbling. Blindness in one eye makes it difficult to judge distances, and nerve damage prevents me from feeling my feet, so sometimes I trip over the funniest things. My limitations, however, remind me that I am also not as strong as I would like to be, emotionally, intellectually, or spiritually.

We are all profoundly deficient and stumble badly spiritually. Even in our prime, we discover that we don't have all the energy and resources we need to face life and all its problems. No matter how qualified or how talented we might be, our nature is inadequate and corrupted. And we can't fix it by trying to be God.

This verse is especially appropriate now, in contemporary U.S. culture, when there is such a lauding of youthfulness. Old people are no longer respected for their wisdom, but are often deposited instead in convalescent centers and left to be lonely. Advertisements pressure us to dress in youthful styles and buy products that will keep us looking young, to use the language of the young and adopt their fads in order to get real "gusto" out of life. Even churches want youthful pastors and discard the old hymns and forms of worship without thinking.

At a professional counselors convention at which I recently spoke, a psychologist clarified the threat to our society that this emphasis on youth poses. An escalating percentage of U.S. citizens are remaining adolescent in their attitudes, behavior, work habits, and family life skills. Needing constantly to be entertained, they remain stuck in the impetuosity, the superficiality, and the immaturity of youth. In contrast, Isaiah 40 invites us not to immaturity but to weakness — availability to and flexibility with God, instead of undisciplined self-centeredness.

Our culture militates against a theology of weakness, for society is built upon seeking after power. We crave influence over others; we work hard to establish our reputations; we manipulate and exploit others to have our own way. The "original" sin was just such a longing for power. In contrast, God calls us to give up our efforts at control. In the truest weakness is seen the truest vision of the grace of God.

Verse 30 emphasizes that our search for strength cannot be a joint effort in which we perform our part and then need God to do a little more to help us. All our strength — and abilities and life — is a gift to us in the first place. We cannot furnish *any* of it on our own.

How does this awareness help us in particular moments of daily life? It enables us to give up trying to stir up our own strength. I'm always amazed that, no matter how tired I am when

I begin teaching Scripture, as soon as I begin to talk about the Word, a new energy is available to me. It's not anything that I can crank up. Much to the contrary, I usually find myself more exhausted before I begin than when my work is finished. Time after time, God's Word is so mighty that it not only carries itself but also carries me with it. I wind up with more energy and Joy than before I began to teach. The LORD's strength is refreshing!

God has repeatedly promised that such things will happen, not only because of the efficacy of his Word, but also because of the nature of his power at work within us. Ephesians 3:20-21a praises God so splendidly in these words: "Now to him who by the power at work within us is able to accomplish abundantly far more than all we can ask or imagine, to him be glory. . . ." Eugene Peterson's *The Message* offers this arresting paraphrase of those expressions and their context:

> My response is to get down on my knees before the Father, this magnificent Father who parcels out all heaven and earth. I ask him to strengthen you by his Spirit — not a brute strength but a glorious inner strength — that Christ will live in you as you open the door and invite him in. And I ask him that with both feet planted firmly on love, you'll be able to take in with all Christians the extravagant dimensions of Christ's love. Reach out and experience the breadth! Test its length! Plumb the depths! Rise to the heights! Live full lives, full in the fullness of God.
>
> God can do anything, you know — far more than you could ever imagine or guess or request in your wildest dreams! He does it not by pushing us around but by working within us, his Spirit deeply and gently within us.[1]

1. Eugene H. Peterson, *The Message: New Testament with Psalms and Proverbs* (Colorado Springs, CO: NavPress, 1995), p. 480.

Beyond our wildest desires, prayers, or hopes — what a promise! Far more abundantly than we could ever experience by ourselves, even in our youth — this is the kind of power that God makes available to us. But knowing that we are hopelessly weak is the first step toward receiving God's gift of might and strength.

QUESTIONS FOR FURTHER MEDITATION:

1. How does my culture accentuate the glories of youth?

2. What are the inadequacies of youth?

3. How do spiritually young people — and churches — stumble and fall?

4. How can I help myself and others admit our inadequacies and accept our limitations?

5. How do I receive the power of God to be active in and through my life?

6. How can the Christian community counteract the increasing tendency of people in our culture to remain adolescent?

7. How can the emphasis of this verse be an encouragement for people past their prime who no longer feel useful in life?

31 *The Cry to Wait*

But those who wait for the LORD shall renew their strength,
they shall mount up with wings like eagles,
they shall run and not be weary,
they shall walk and not faint.

Isaiah 40:31

He poured out his ecstasy on the piano. A tremendous burden of guilt had been lifted when he confessed his sin and received God's forgiveness. His gifted playing was characterized now by the power of freedom, and new creative energies were released. After the counseling session, I listened from the narthex of the church until suddenly he came running out and asked me to put a text to his melody. His exquisite music then carried these inadequate words:

The storm has passed; the skies grow clear.
Soon all is well when God is near.

Winds may still toss; waves crash on shores,
But in God's hands the eagle soars!

I shall mount up on eagle's wings;
I overcome when my heart sings,

"Thanks be to God" for victories
Over my sin. Forgiveness frees!

The last verse of Isaiah 40 provided the image for that song twenty years ago. The picture of soaring eagles continues to be one of my favorite expressions for the freedom and strength God gives to those who have grown faint and weary from the burdens of worry and fear, guilt and sin. Such weightlessness is available to all who wait upon the LORD.

Verse 31 begins with a Hebrew grammatical form that emphasizes the relationship of the LORD with those who wait upon him. Actually the phrase reads, "those waiters-upon of *YHWH*." The form does not necessarily accentuate that they belong to him (although that is true), but rather that they depend upon him in a special way.

When I first wrote this chapter, I had recently traveled two hours south to study with my Hebrew professor. On the way to the seminary, I stopped at a Christian bookstore to buy him a present, but the store was not yet open. I had to wait for the clerks to unlock the doors if I wanted to purchase the gift I had in mind. My action couldn't be taken until they acted first.

Similarly, we are "waiters-upon" of the LORD. We look to him in faith for the fulfillment of his promises. We believe in his power and recognize that all our abilities and strengths are first his gifts. No action can be taken on our part until he has acted first out of the abundance of his grace.

Those who do such waiting, the prophet promises, "shall renew their strength." The verb actually means "to change it for the better, to substitute it," perhaps even "to exchange it" as one replaces one's attire. In other words, we can turn in our deficient strength and take the LORD's instead. The word translated "strength" is the same one that is the last of four terms in verse 26 and the first of the repetitions in verse 29. Its use again here reminds us of all the things we learned when we meditated upon those verses.

Verse 31 concludes with three pictures of the results from that exchange of strength. First, "they shall mount up on pinions as eagles." The verb is the same one we met in verse 9 and means "to rise or go up," even as the pilgrims went up to the temple, and it is in an imperfect form, which stresses continuous action. We shall continually ascend as we wait upon *YHWH*.

The word for "pinions" is a fascinating choice. It is derived from a verb that speaks of strength and is related to many words meaning "mighty" or "valiant." The modern Hebrew words for "air force" and "airplane" are derived from the same root. Thus, inherent in the picture of the eagles' wings is an added impression of extra strength and power.

The last two phrases make use of the poetic device of chiasm, in which two items in sequence are then repeated in reverse order (*a b b a*). The two terms "to become faint" and "to grow weary" were used in verse 28 to describe their absence in the God of everlastingness. Then, in verses 29 and 30, they were used to show that human beings who are the opposite of God possess them. Now the terms are reversed to emphasize this ending: Those who wait upon the LORD no longer experience growing weary and becoming faint. In addition, the verb is imperfect and shows continuing action. Thus, the prophet's final point is conclusively made: "they shall run and not be weary; they shall walk and not faint." Period. Exclamation point!

We have seen in the fortieth chapter of Isaiah many important lessons concerning our daily lives as Christians. Verse 31 seems to bring them all together with seven important themes. The first four are presented by particular words or phrases; the last three come from the pictures that show what our lives can become when God is thoroughly in control.

The most important word around which the verse — and the chapter and the entire book of Isaiah — is focused is the name *YHWH*. What kind of God do we have? We have seen in previous verses many aspects of his character, but we remember especially in connection with the term *YHWH* that he is a covenant God, a gracious and compassionate God, who wills the very best for us. Because he is that kind of God, he enables us to be "waiters-upon" of him. We long to deepen our experience of waiting because we believe in him as LORD of our lives.

The second theme is the waiting itself. We wait hopeful- ly — with a hope that does not disappoint (Romans 5:5) — because we know that, in his time and according to his perfect wisdom, the LORD brings all things together for good to those who love him (8:28). We often wait restlessly, so we need the community of faithful people to help us learn to abide with greater trust and confidence. The word *wait* implies absolute realization that the LORD is in control, that in his sovereignty God will accomplish his purposes, which are best for us. There- fore, thinking about the kind of God we have, envisioning the immensity of his power and love, and knowing that he alone is the God of everlastingness, we await his perfect will. We want to want only what he wants. That causes us to depend on him, to expect his perfect timing, and thereby to act in accordance with his revelation.

What will happen when we wait in such a way? The third emphasis of this verse is that our strength will be renewed. Not usually associated with this verse, the second meaning of the Hebrew word usually translated "renew" is "to be exchanged." We don't just pep up our own strength; we don't merely supplement it. Rather, we turn it in for that which is truly strong, a power that is new. Our human strength is totally insufficient, and so we have to uncover something previously unknown. In Christ we start all over with the transformation that makes everything a new creation (2 Corinthians 5:17).

When we exchange our strength, we don't receive the kind of power the world offers and fights for. We don't receive more blatant might, but we receive "a spirit of power and love and self-control" (2 Timothy 1:7, RSV). The combination of those three gifts enables us to understand the unique kind of potency God wants us to exert. His power is governed by love, intelligent and purposeful love directed toward the needs of others, and then further channeled by self-control. This kind of strength reaches out to others and is directed toward their needs, toward the upbuilding and extending of the Kingdom of God.

The kind of strength received is the fourth theme of the chapter summarized in this verse. When we wait before the LORD, it is not to receive power only for ourselves, but so that God's purposes can be accomplished for the building up of his Body and the renewing of his Kingdom. We wait to exchange our humanness for God's love, operative through us with all its power. We wait for the renewing of our spirits by the gift of his. We wait to be transformed, to become more and more like the image of his Son, Jesus Christ.

This leads us to the final three pictures — three inspiring images of the fullness, satisfaction, and completeness of life in the LORD. The first representation is that we shall mount up with pinions like eagles. Perhaps you have watched eagles gloriously soaring with their incredible power and grace — continually mounting up, gliding with such apparent ease. When we wait before *YHWH*, we, too, rise up above our troubles. Winds may still toss, and waves crash on shores, but in God's hands the eagle soars! The storms of this life will continue to buffet us, but in the midst of them we find ourselves surmounting them or enduring them or transforming them. We are as pilgrims, ascending the holy hill to worship at the LORD's temple. Having his strength empowers us, in spite of obstacles, to experience his perfect grace at work in and through us. We shall mount up with pinions of strength; we shall be like the eagles in their freedom.

Then we are given a new perspective. The eagle sees from high above the earth. That is the vision offered when Ephesians 2:6 declares that we are "seated . . . with him in the heavenly places in Christ Jesus" or when Colossians 3:2 urges us to "set [our] minds on things that are above." By waiting on the LORD, we climb up to view things from his perspective, to get the bigger picture. We can see beyond the limits of our present existence into God's larger purposes, not only for our particular lives, but also for the whole Church and for everything by which he will be glorified.

The second picture in this verse is that we shall run and not be weary. Two friends who are runners asked me to use this verse for their wedding sermon, and preparations for that occasion suggested to me that this image could imply training and discipline. Runners such as the heralds in verse 9 were seasoned to carry their message speedily and with endurance. As we continue to wait before the LORD, he increases our endurance so that more and more we can run and not be weary. What a contrast this is to the previous verse, which warns that even young men shall fall exhausted. Verse 31 promises that the exchange of our strength for God's equips us for the long haul, the big pushes.

The last picture is that we shall walk and not faint. This picture seems to imply steadiness; it suggests consistency of life. The word *walk* is often used in the Scriptures with the connotation of our daily behavior or course of conduct. If we walk continually in the LORD, we shall not lose the way or lose heart or become discouraged.

When I first wrote this book, a friend of mine had recently climbed to the top of Mount Rainier for the first time. He said that the important thing in such a long climb was for the team to keep moving up, slowly but surely. This last verse invites us to that constancy in our Christian faith, to continue enduring the necessary struggles of daily life and, through it all, to keep on walking consistently in our relationship with *YHWH* as we move together toward the goal.

My friend told me after his return from Mount Rainier of the exhilaration of reaching the top, even in a blizzard, and of being hardly able to realize that he had actually made it. It was very disappointing, then, that because of the storm, his team had to come back down immediately. The hope of our walk as Christians is that we are also moving toward the top. We are on our way to meeting *YHWH* there, face to face. But when we arrive, we won't ever have to come back down. Now it is our purpose to keep on walking and not to faint. It is our exchanged strength that enables us to do that.

Moving on our way toward heaven through this life, the permanence of our final ascent gives us a crucial assurance. Because it is so difficult to keep going sometimes, it is extremely comforting to know that we will indeed make it by God's grace. This picture promises us that we shall walk and not faint, and our sure trust in God's promises characterizes all our Christian life. We know we can overcome all obstacles because God has begun his work in our lives, and he has promised to bring that work to completion until the day of Jesus Christ (Philippians 1:6).

We shall walk and not faint because we wait upon *YHWH*. We have exchanged our feeble strength for his own; we are filled with his Spirit for the walking. We move toward the goal of the upward call of God in Jesus Christ (Philippians 3:14) and toward the time of knowing the LORD face to face. Ultimately, that is what we wait for, and while we wait we move. While we wait, we live in a world that needs to recognize all the cries of our human weaknesses and yearnings and all the answering cries of *YHWH*'s Truth, which satisfies all our deepest desires.

QUESTIONS FOR FURTHER MEDITATION:

1. What obstacles in my life frustrate my waiting?

2. What kinds of doubts do I have about the character of the LORD?

3. Why is it so hard for me to wait for God's timing?

4. What might be the problem in those moments when I don't realize the strength of the LORD *in my life?*

5. How can the promises of this verse motivate me in difficult times?

6. How could my Christian community better equip me for the running and the walking?

7. How has this chapter from Isaiah changed my life as I have studied it?